simple knits for easy living

simple knits for easy living

erika knight

PHOTOGRAPHY BY JOHN HESELTINE

COLLINS & BROWN

This book is dedicated to generation Y2K,

hopefully to inspire a little homespun creativity

in a high-tech world!

First published in Great Britain in 2000 by
Collins & Brown Limited
The Chrysalis Building
Bramley Road, London W10 6SP

Distributed in the United States and Canada by Sterling Publishing
Co., 387 Park Avenue South, New York, NY 10016, USA

British Library Cataloguing-in-Publication Data:
A catalogue record for this title is available from the British Library.

1 3 5 7 9 8 6 4 2
ISBN 1 85585 772 3
A BERRY BOOK
Conceived, edited and designed by Susan Berry, in association with
Debbie Mole and Erika Knight, for Collins & Brown
Design and Art Direction: Debbie Mole
Editor: Sally Harding

Reproduction by Classic Scan, Singapore
Printed and bound by Kyodo, Singapore

contents listing

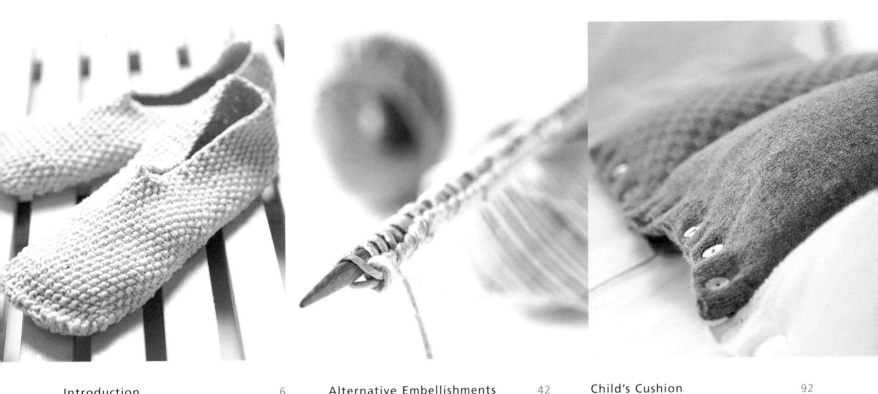

bathing

living

sleeping

knitting is simple

Take two smooth wooden sticks and a continuous length of 'yarn', and in four simple steps ~ **in, over, under, off** ~ make a **stitch**. Make several stitches to make a **row**. Make several rows to make a **fabric.** This books aims to **take the pain out of knitting.** Forget complex knitting patterns. Here we go, **back to the very basics** with **simple language · no abbreviations · no difficult shaping · no charts or diagrams to follow · no tension rules.** Knitted pieces **based on simple rectangles** are **easy to knit, speedy to knit.** To begin, just learn to cast on, knit two basic stitches and cast off. It is all you need to know. Simple stitches in simple shapes and simple yarns create beautiful pieces for every day of your life and **for every room in your home** ~ for living · for sleeping · for bathing.

For sheer pleasure, I like to use **bamboo knitting needles** ~ light, sleek and smooth. They are beautiful to look at and beautiful to the touch, and they allow the knitting to slide. Experiment with the feel of natural materials from string to cashmere. Try them all ~ wool, cotton, linen, sisal, mohair, chenille. **'Feel' the different textures.** Then add to the fun by experimenting with **non-traditional materials** ~ wire, nylon, twine, rags, cloth tapes and raffia. Knitting creates a **back-to-basics aesthetic.** It is a **nurturing craft** and an honest one. Today, giving something hand-made and personalised is both a caring act and **the ultimate in luxury and chic.** Just get going, break the rules. Take pleasure using texture and creating something by hand that is **simple, beautiful and easy.**

enjoy

yarns : natural wood

NATURAL WOOD TONES: For inspiration for colour in your knitting, look to natural, hard materials such as wood, stone, slate, steel and glass. They each have their own inherent palette of hues, which comfortably contrast and coexist with softer cotton, linen, wool, leather, suede and textiles to create a home rich in surface textures. The timeless neutrals provided by these rich natural elements are highlighted by earth and vegetable tones, as well as indigos and whites. On this and the following pages I explore some

1: Parcel string – Simple, basic, functional and inexpensive, parcel string is also rich in tone and texture.

2: Sisal string – Coarse and naturally abrasive, sisal adds authenticity to simple pieces or details.

3 & 4: Cotton yarns – Naturally dry and soft, cotton yarns are available in a wide variety of tones and textures. Fine cotton is beautifully refined when worked in simple textures like moss stitch.

5: Garden twines – Like sisal, garden twine is rough and rustic, but more pliable.

of these combinations as sources for selecting yarns for simple, beautiful projects for the home.

Natural wood is a good starting point for design ideas. From worn bark, to weathered surfaces, smoothly polished cork and honey-coloured floors, wood is rich in warm colour and tone. Wood, rough or smooth, is naturally complemented by the simple textures of coarse yellow sisal string, fine ivory-coloured parcel string, rough garden twine, smooth classic ecru cotton yarns and grainy buttons.

yarns : **stone & steel**

1: **Alpaca** – Soft, warm alpaca is rich in natural tones.

2: **Mélange yarns** – Contrasting strands twisted together form unique yarn mixtures.

3: **Leather string** – Matt, smooth leather string complements the stone and steel theme.

4: **Chenille** – A velvet-textured cotton.

5: **Felted yarn** – Light, voluminous lofty wool.

6: **Bouclé** – An airy, lightweight looped or curled woollen yarn.

7: **Synthetic fibres** – Transparent, pearlised man-made threads add surface contrast.

STONE & STEEL TONES: Like natural wood, stone and steel is a fertile source of colour inspiration. Here shades of stone, pebble and pearl are balanced with natural shadows of steel, slate and carbon.

Matt, smooth, grainy or polished, absolute neutrals – tone on tone – create a classic elegant modern interior. For this theme, soft alpaca in subtle natural tones, yarns with mélanges of tone and texture, luxurious quick-to-knit felted wool and curly textured bouclé create voluminous, lofty and weightless fabrics. To counter and complement this, smooth leather, velvety chenille and pearlised transparent nylons add a unique harder edge to a simple contemporary look. Consider authentic troche pearl buttons for finishing touches; they reflect the subtle tints and hues of greys, making them a natural choice where quality is not compromised.

yarns : **soft suede**

SOFT SUEDE TONES: The themes of soft suede and smooth leather are good illustrations of how simple textural differences alter our view of colour. Texture can soften or sharpen by its depths of shadows or strength of hightlights. Suede here inspires softly blurred textures that add an elegantly plump yet comfortable 'Sunday'

1: Merino – Soft, light and airy wool yarn.
2: Bouclé – Curly yarn effective for simple cushions and throws.
3: Chenille – Velvety cotton, luxurious in both

fine and fat weights.
4: Angora – Ultra fine, extremely soft yarn from the angora rabbit.
5: Cashmere – A yarn that is the ultimate natural classic luxury.

feeling to any living space – yarns that feel as beautiful as they look and that are warm and sensual to the touch. Smooth, rounded merino wool and precious and intimate blends of angora, alpaca, cashmere and mohair create downy suede surfaces in a delicate, sophisticated palette of biscuit, blonde, palomino and butter.

yarns : leather

LEATHER TONES: The leather theme here gives rise to an evocative mix of smooth, hard polished surfaces and luxuriously soft cashmere, velvet-touch fine and fat chenille, and slippery silks. Warm shades of browns – from subtle rosy taupe and milk chocolate, via mocha and deep aubergine, through to rich teak and oak – create

1: Chunky chenille – This fat, velvet-like yarn complements smooth leather beautifully.

2: Fine chenille – Less textured than the fat chenille when knitted.

3: Silk yarns – The queen of fibres, silk is warm and fluid. Equally elegant, but softer and with a more subtle lustre, cashmere would also suit this theme.

a comfortable, cultivated and eclectic mood. Precise and refined details in knitted fabrics contrasted with smooth, hard finishing touches like dark wood buttons add elegance and quality to simple pieces.

yarns : earth

EARTH TONES: Natural earth tones inspire a new look at neutrals. Add living warmth to surface and texture in the home with a rhythmic mix of vigorous greens – algae, lichen and moss – and earthy taupe and peat. Rustic tweed-effect yarns and chunky tweeds, coordinate with cotton, chenille, silk and natural linen for a rich

1: Chenille – Velvety chenille blends well with the organic theme.

2: Cotton – Smooth or rustic, fat or fine.

3: Silk – Delicate, smooth, satiny fibre.

4: Tweed – Provides instant texture through mixed colour.

5: Ridge textures – Purl-stitch ridges add texture.

6: Linen – A cool, dry ancient rustic yarn.

depth of colour and a sense of warmth and protection. This look can be further enhanced with 'rough' reverse-stocking-stitch and purl-stitch ridges, and detailed with authentic horn buttons. Earth tone and texture combinations are unexpectedly modern in their application for home decoration.

yarns:vegetable

VEGETABLE TONES: The absolute classic and timeless neutrals shown on the previous pages are highlighted by seasonal earth hues as well as by these vegetable tones. Derived from the primal essential ingredients for everyday living, vegetable colours provide creative sustenance for the seasonal home. Fresh fleshy figs, tender

1: Merino and cotton mix – Mixing cotton and wool in a yarn creates an ideal smoothness and elasticity.

2: Chunky chenille – Soft, velvety chenille comes in a range of vegetal tones.

3: Fine chenille – Thinner weights of chenille produce smoother knitted fabrics than the thicker ones.

pink shoots of aromatic basil, pale leafy ribs of celery, mauvy tips of young asparagus prove how often intense tones of colour easily coexist in nature. Velvety chenille, both fine and fat, and mixed yarn made from soft merino wool and cotton fibres supply the vegetable shades that bring life to this design story.

yarns : indigo & denim

INDIGO AND DENIM TONES: Casual, easy and relaxed, tones of indigo, denim and chambray are modern 'neutrals' for any room in the home. Indigo is an ancient natural dye that has been used to colour cotton for thousands of years.

The popularity of indigo is based on its extraordinary quality to fade gradually and age naturally and beautifully with wear. In its many permutations, indigo is evocative of sun-bleached beaches and the seashore – a mood you

1: Mid-blue denim yarn – The traditional unwashed mid-blue denim hue.

2: Stone-washed denim yarn – The shade of gracefully faded indigo.

3: Dark blue denim yarn – A deep, dark indigo tone.

4: Off-white denim yarn – Stone, off-white and ecru shades provide contrast to the blues.

5: Chenille – A soft complement for cool, smooth cotton yarns.

6: Cotton yarn – Shiny or matt cottons fit perfectly into the denim look.

can take into your interiors by making cushions and throws with denim knitting yarn. This yarn is 100 per cent cotton and knits into a slightly firmer, weightier fabric than other cotton yarns. Denim yarns in shades of indigo offset with basic natural tones of ecru and stone create casual classic designs.

Both velvety chenille and smooth and matt cotton yarns in cool blues and warmer off-whites will enhance the overall indigo theme.

yarns : white

1: Merino – This soft wool yarn is good for refined knitted detail.

2: Merino and cotton mix – A mixed merino wool and cotton yarn, extra soft, yet cool.

3: Raffia – Cast-on and cast-off edges in raffia add a modern texture.

4: Cord – Use to trim or accessorise knits.

5: Rag knit – Strips of terry, muslin and net, and lengths of raffia, bouclé, chenille and cord all knitted together.

6: Fine cotton – Smooth cotton yarns accentuate stitch patterns.

WHITE: Absolutely essential to any home are whites. Implacable, indispensable, fresh, clean and calming, they ground the neutral palette. White is the colour of total order, yet it is rich in diversity of texture and tone – frosty textures of glass and ice, transluscent mother-of-pearl, chalky soft chenille, fine piquet cottons, whisper-light wool, milky white muslin, opaque nylon and papery raffia. Textured whites translate into the finest or coarsest of knits.

equipment

TOOLS & MATERIALS: The equipment required to make any of the projects in this book is simple, inexpensive and readily available. Here are some of the basics to start you off.

yarn: First, you will need knitting yarn. You do not have to restrict yourself to the conventional either! There are many materials that, although they are not usually used for knitting, will do just as well. For example, string, ribbon, tape, twine, wire, felt – in fact, you can knit practically anything you want that is flexible enough.

knitting needles: These are available in a variety of sizes from fine to fat. My favourite type are bamboo, which are beautiful to work with as they are light and smooth and allow the knitting to slide. They also look great reclining on your settee or throw or embedded in some wonderful textile, should a friend call round unexpectedly.

tape measure or ruler: You'll need this for measuring knitting as you proceed.

scissors: For cutting yarn or loose ends on knitting, a sharp pair of scissors is a must.

glass-headed pins: Pins with glass heads are easy to spot when sewing up your knitting – you'll be sure not to leave any behind.

sewing needle: Use large blunt-ended needles to sew your knitting together with yarn.

buttons: When projects are so simple, the detailing is crucial. Buttons are perfect for use as simple but effective highlights, so keep them in mind and choose them carefully when finishing off your knitting.

cork: A wine cork is handy for sticking needle tips into, to prevent stitches from falling off, and to prevent sharp points from poking through if you travel with your knitting like I do.

bag: Lastly, find a suitable bag for keeping knitting clean and carrying it with you.

techniques

TENSION: Don't stress about the word 'tension'. It simply means that by changing the size of your knitting needles, you can control the size of your knitting. As a basic rule *fine needles go with fine yarn and fat needles with fat yarn.* You can see here the difference in size of the stitches when this rule is applied (right). The secret to getting the best from any yarn is to experiment to discover the best size needle to use with a particular yarn. You could knit up several yarns in an evening to find out how easily they knit and the look and feel of the fabric you prefer. The same yarn

fine yarn: fine needles

medium yarn: medium needles

fat yarn: fat needles

medium yarn: fine needles

edium yarn: medium needles

medium yarn: fat needles

knitted on different-size needles looks quite different – from very dense to very loose (left).

If you know the size of each stitch (see page 124), you can make a piece of knitting any width you want, but for most of the simple projects in the following chapters exact size is not important – relax, a few too many or too few stitches will not make much difference. Enjoy the process of knitting and texture – remember, yarns have different qualities, and by using fatter or finer knitting needles you can achieve a fabric that you are happy with.

one : **loop**

Loop the yarn over your left thumb with the ball end on the left and a long end on the right.

CASTING ON: Before you can start knitting, the first thing to do is to 'cast on'. This is the process of making loops or 'stitches' with a length of yarn on one of the knitting needles. Simple! There are many methods for doing this, but one of the easiest is shown here. (See page 30 for how to make a 'knit' cast on at the beginning of a row.) If you haven't tried casting on before, take a little time to practice and it will become automatic after a while. When you start a knitting pattern it will tell you exactly how many stitches to cast on before you begin.

four : **down**

Pull the yarn on the needle down through the loop on your thumb to make the first loop.

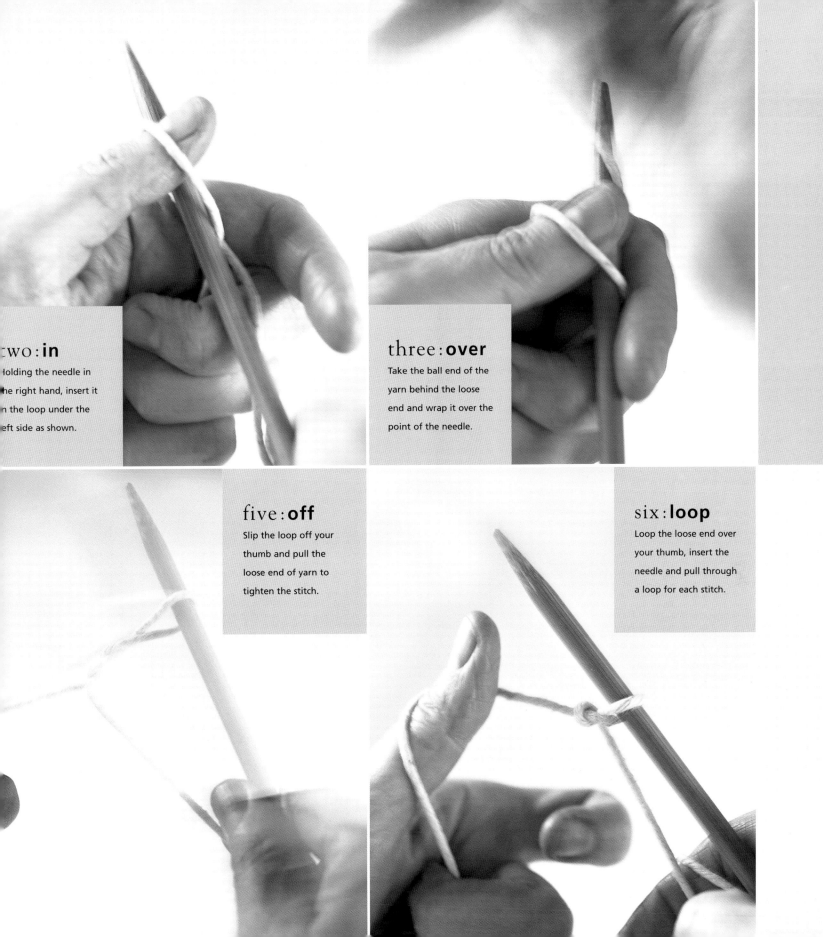

two : **in**

Holding the needle in the right hand, insert it in the loop under the left side as shown.

three : **over**

Take the ball end of the yarn behind the loose end and wrap it over the point of the needle.

five : **off**

Slip the loop off your thumb and pull the loose end of yarn to tighten the stitch.

six : **loop**

Loop the loose end over your thumb, insert the needle and pull through a loop for each stitch.

one: knit 2

To begin casting off, first knit 2 stitches so that there are 2 loops on the right-hand needle.

four: off

Let first stitch drop off the right-hand needle, so only the second stitch remains on it.

CASTING OFF: To finish your piece of knitted fabric so that it will not unravel, you 'cast off' the stitches. This is the process of drawing one stitch loop through the next all along the needle as you knit across a row. When the instructions just say 'cast off' it means to knit each stitch as you cast off. But sometimes it will tell you to 'cast off in pattern', in which case you should knit or purl each stitch in the pattern you were using in the previous rows, as you cast off. Casting off a few stitches within the knitted fabric (and casting on again in the next row to replace the stitches) is also used for buttonholes.

two:in

Insert the point of the left-hand needle in the first stitch on the right-hand needle as shown.

three:over

Lift the first stitch on the right-hand needle over the second stitch on the right-hand needle.

five:repeat

Repeat across the row, knitting next stitch and lifting first stitch over it, until one stitch remains.

six:finish

To finish the cast off, cut working yarn, pull the end through the last loop and tighten.

one: **in**

Insert point of right-hand needle in first stitch on left-hand needle as shown.

MAKING A KNIT STITCH: After casting on the appropriate number of stitches as shown on pages 22 and 23, you can begin your first row of knitting. The knit stitch is made in a simple four-step process as shown here, repeating the steps until all the stitches on the left-hand needle have been transferred to the right-hand needle. Once you have completed the row, transfer the needle holding the worked stitches to your left hand, and begin again with another row of knit stitches, to create a fabric known as garter stitch (shown in close up).

two: **over**

Holding the yarn in the right hand, wrap it over point of right-hand needle to make a loop.

three : under

Pull the new loop on
right-hand needle under
and through first loop on
the left-hand needle.

four : off

Slide stitch off the point
of left-hand needle. You
have now knitted one
stitch onto right needle.

one : **in**

Insert point of right-hand needle in first stitch on left-hand needle as shown.

MAKING A PURL STITCH: The purl stitch is worked in much the same way as the knit stitch, but the yarn is held at the front of the work instead of the back. Knit and purl is all there is to know! Combining these two is the basis of all knitted fabric. Stocking stitch is made by working one row knit and one purl alternately: the right side (or knit side) is smooth and the wrong side (purl) is ridged or rough. When the purl side is the right side, the fabric is called reverse stocking stitch. Other knitted textures are made by using knit and purl stitches in the same row.

two : **over**

Holding the yarn in the right hand, wrap yarn over point of right-hand needle to make a loop.

three : under

Pull the new loop on right-hand needle under and through first loop on the left-hand needle.

four : off

Slide stitch off the point of left-hand needle, leaving new purled stitch on right needle.

one:**in**

To increase by 'casting on', insert right-hand needle in first stitch and pull a loop through.

two:**in**

Do not drop stitch from left needle. Insert left needle in new loop and slip it off right needle.

three:**on**

You now have an extra stitch on the left-hand needle. Begin the next row in the usual way.

INCREASING: Adding or taking away stitches from a row will shape your knitting. These techniques are called 'increasing' and 'decreasing' and are used to shape the slippers on page 96. One of the simplest ways of adding stitches is to 'cast on' new loops at the end of a row in the same way you do when starting to knit (see page 22) or to work a 'knit' cast on at the beginning of a row as shown here. An equally simple increase technique is to knit into the front, then back of the same stitch before slipping it off the left-hand needle – making two from one.

one : **in**

Insert right-hand needle in two stitches (through front or back loops) and wrap yarn over needle.

two : **under**

With two stitches still on left-hand needle, pull yarn under and through both stitches at once.

three : **off**

Drop two stitches from left-hand needle. You have just made two stitches into one.

DECREASING: One way to reduce the number of stitches in a row is to 'cast off' stitches in the same way you finish off a row of knitting (see page 24). This creates a little ledge on the edge of the knitting, so if you only want to decrease one stitch at the side of your knitting and make a smooth slant, a better and simpler method is to knit (or purl) two stitches together. This is done by inserting the right-hand needle through two stitches on the left-hand needle at the same time (either through the front or back of the loops) and knitting them both off at once.

living

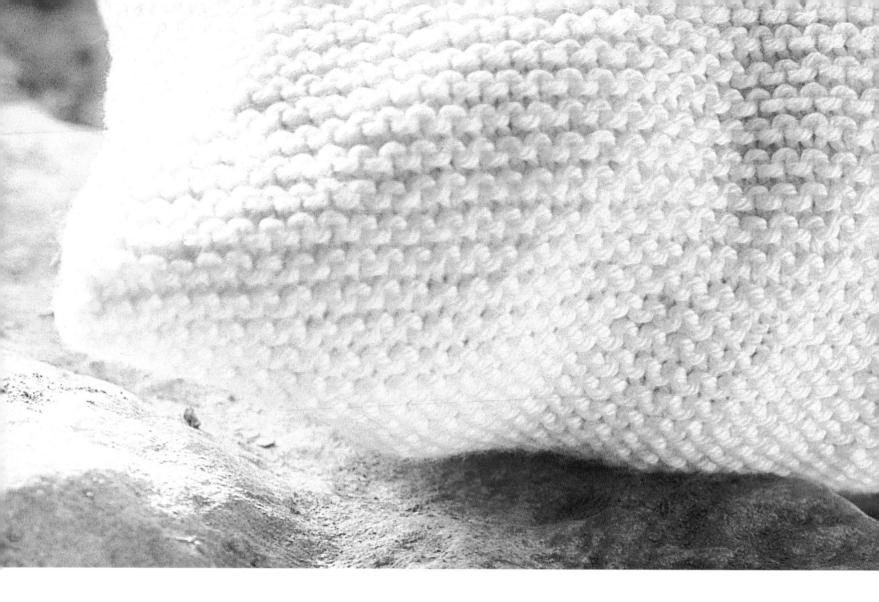

simple cushions : cotton or chenille

Knitted in cotton or chenille yarn in garter stitch, this cushion has a beautiful raised texture. No

increasing, difficult shaping or tricky finishing details are needed. Its simplicity is its major design

feature: it is a straight length of knitting, folded twice, and then simply seamed together. This clean-

cut style allows the yarn qualities to shine, so varying the kind of yarn has a big effect on its look

and feel. Chenille gives a much softer, more luxurious finish to the cushion than the natural, cool

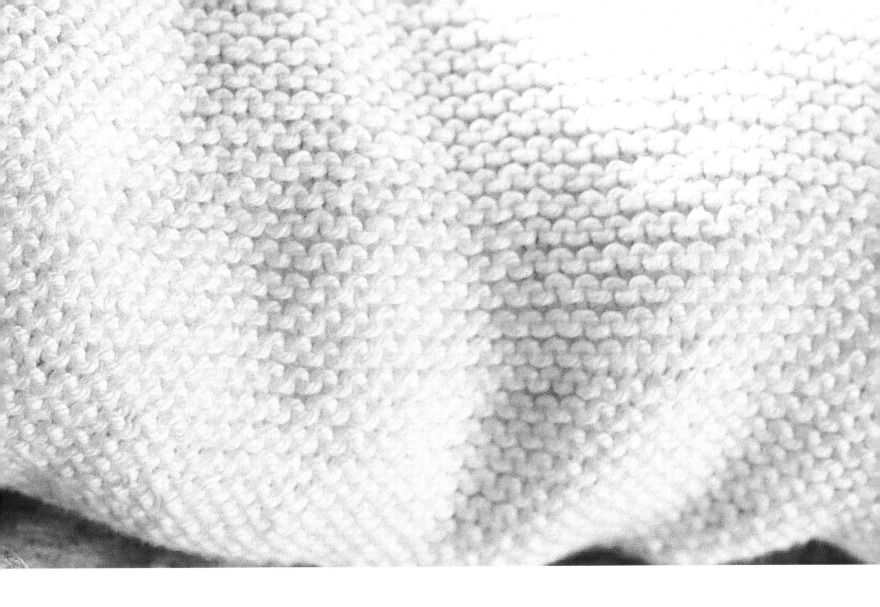

cotton. You could also try working it in ultra-tactile yarns like alpaca or cashmere. Or use a soft string

for a more contemporary, crisper finish. Neutral colours – cream, ecru, beige and off-white – serve

to emphasise the textural resonances of the yarn. Several cushions in toning shades will complement

each other. The cushion here measures 50cm (20in) square, but you can create whatever size cushion

you like by following the simple calculation guide on page 124.

how to make : simple cushions

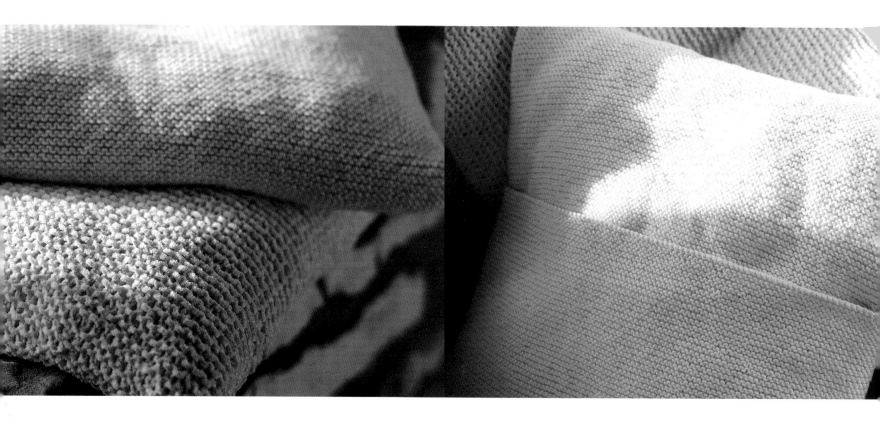

FOR THE SIMPLE COTTON CUSHION: Use 10 x 50g balls Rowan *Handknit D.K. Cotton*, pair 4mm needles, sewing needle and pins, 50cm-square feather cushion pad

METHOD FOR THE SIMPLE COTTON CUSHION *(worked in one piece)*: Using 4mm needles, cast on 100 stitches. Work 28cm in garter stitch (knit every row). Tie a coloured piece of yarn at the start and finish of the next row – this will show where to fold later. Work in garter stitch for another 50cm. Tie a coloured piece of yarn at the start and finish of the next row. Work in garter stitch until the fabric measures 106cm in total. Cast off.

FINISHING: To sew the cushion together, lay the knitting out flat (gently steam it with an iron at this stage). Then

above left: The simple cotton cushion seen on top of the chenille cushion emphasises the softer, loftier texture of the chenille yarn.

above right: The back of the cotton cushion shows the simple envelope finish.

opposite: An essay in texture – the two cushions in different yarns, but knitted in the same simple garter stitch, contrasting with a loosely woven throw.

fold the work in from the first set of coloured markers and stitch the two layers together at each side using yarn and a fine running stitch or backstitch. Now fold knitting in from second set of markers and stitch the seams as before, sewing through all thicknesses of the overlapping pieces to make an 'envelope'. Turn right side out and place cushion pad inside.

FOR THE SIMPLE CHENILLE CUSHION: Use 5 x 100g balls Rowan *Chunky Cotton Chenille*, pair 5mm needles, sewing needle and pins, 50cm-square feather cushion pad

METHOD FOR THE SIMPLE CHENILLE CUSHION: Using 5mm needles, cast on 75 stitches. Work in garter stitch following the instructions for the simple cotton cushion.

seams cushion : textured squares

This cushion is the ultimate in texture and the quickest knit ever! You just have to try knitting it.

Cosy and comfortable, the yarn is thick and softly bulky, yet so very light and airy. The cushion is

knitted on fat needles and worked in small manageable sections approximately 19cm (7½in) square,

which makes it an ideal project to begin with as you can watch it grow! The finished blocks are

arranged with the 'smooth' and 'rough' sides of the fabric alternating in an update of popular

patchwork. The blocks are joined with outside seams to give a modern detail to this fashionably felted home accessory. Several cushions in tonal shades of charcoal greys would be a cosy accompaniment nestling side by side in a contemporary or rustic living space. For a hint of colour, you could oversew the seams in a highlight shade. Or use one of the simple alternative embroidery embellishments shown on pages 42 and 43 in a highlight colour to give a seasonal accent.

how to make: **seams cushion**

FOR THE SEAMS CUSHION: Use 9 x 50g balls Rowan *Chunky Soft*, pair 7mm needles, sewing needle and pins, 55cm-square feather cushion pad

METHOD FOR THE SEAMS CUSHION: THE FRONT: Using 7mm needles, cast on 21 stitches. Work in stocking stitch (knit 1 row and purl the next alternately) for a total of 19cm. Cast off. Work another 8 squares in stocking stitch in exactly the same way.

THE BACK: Using 7mm needles, cast on 61 sts. Work in garter stitch (knit every row) for a total of 6cm – this will give a firm edge. Now change to stocking stitch (knit 1 row and purl 1 row alternately) and work until the knitting measures a total of 33cm. Cast off. Make another piece in exactly the same way.

above left: Simply 'pinch' the two pieces together to start the seam, pin, and sew.

above centre: Position the squares together with the 'smooth' and the 'rough' sides alternating.

above right: The back is knitted in two pieces that overlap.

opposite: Simple squares of knitting are seamed on the outside to give a textured look.

FINISHING: Lay out the 9 squares for the front in a grid 3 squares wide by 3 squares deep. You will notice that there is a 'smooth' side and a 'rough' side or textured side to the knitting. Reposition the 'squares' so that the 'smooth' side and the 'rough' side of the knitting are alternate. You may wish to press the squares slightly at this stage, with a steam iron, to keep flat. Thread a large needle with the yarn and sew the squares together using a fine running stitch or backstitch. Now take the 2 pieces for the back and gently steam flat. Place pieces so that the garter stitch edges overlap one another to make a back 55cm square and so that one piece has the 'smooth' side facing upwards and the other the 'rough' side; pin in position. Finally, sew the front and back together around the outer edge with all the seams on the outside. Insert the cushion pad.

swatches:embellishments

ALTERNATIVE EMBELLISHMENTS: It is very easy to embellish your knitting. It does not have to be anything intricate, complicated or ornate; there are many ways to embroider or decorate with simple techniques. The most basic stitches inspire a variety of ideas.

Top left: Use a contrasting colour of the same yarn and simply stitch diagonally in and out in running stitch across the fabric. Then go back and work a second row of stitches beside the first, keeping them irregular and 'sketchy' for a rustic feel. **Top centre:** For an effective hand-made or ethnic look, oversew along the join of two different colours or textures in a hightlight colour.

Top right: With a contrasting or tonal colour or texture use a regular running stitch to make a large cross in the middle of large squares. **Bottom left:** Outside seams look modern and functional. These could be oversewn for further effect in a contrasting or tonal colour. **Bottom centre:** Using several strands of coloured yarn, sew in and out leaving long loops on the surface. Then cut the loops, knot and trim. **Bottom right:** Basic cross stitch is beautifully simple on reverse textures.

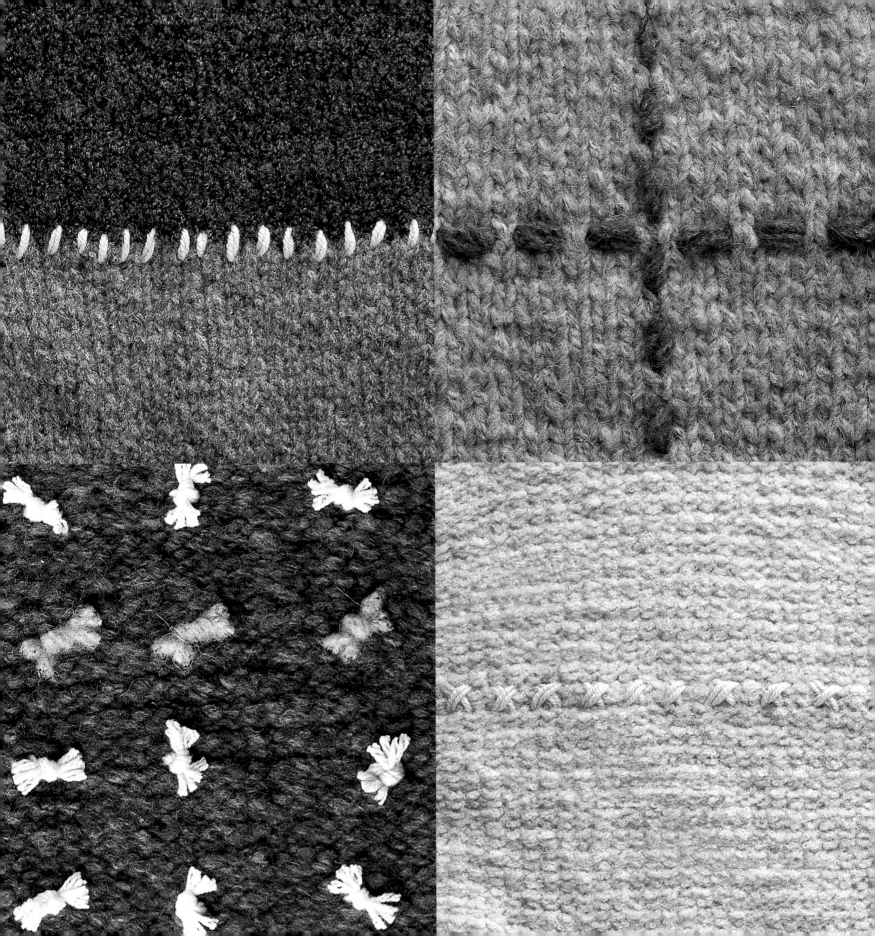

stripe cushion : string and chenille

Add stripes to your knitting! Two random strips of natural-coloured string add interest to the front

of a simple contemporary cushion, especially when worked in reverse stocking stitch. The string gives

a textural irregularity to the stripes and contrasts beautifully with the luxurious velvety pile of the

tonal-coloured cotton chenille fabric. Adding stripes is a very easy technique: at the beginning of a

row just join in a new ball or length of colour – the ends can be knotted or sewn into the back on

completion. Play with stripes in your knitting. If you change colours when working in stocking stitch, the stripes will have a continuous smooth edge. But if you change shades when working in reverse stocking stitch, the purl stitch on the right side of the fabric will produce an interesting broken line of colour. The same number of rows can be used for each colour or varied to give an uneven stripe repeat. The simplest line of contrasting colour or texture can be amazingly effective.

how to make: stripe cushion

Chenille (1 strand only) and continue in stocking stitch until the knitted piece measures a total of 114cm from cast-on edge. Change to 2 strands dark brown *Fine Chenille* and work 1 more row, then cast off all the stitches firmly.

FINISHING: Measure and mark two fold lines on the knitted piece – one 32cm from the cast-off edge (along the dark brown line) and the second 32cm in from the cast-on edge. With right sides of fabric facing, fold along the marked lines making sure that the dark brown cast-off edge is under the light brown cast-on edge. The two ends overlap by about 14cm. Sew the sides of the cushion cover together through all the thicknesses, using yarn and either a fine backstitch or a fine running stitch. Turn right side out and insert the cushion pad.

left: A stripe of string accents the velvety chenille.

top right: Purl on the right side with a new colour to create a broken line.

bottom right: The opening on the cushion back has a contrasting cast-off edge.

FOR THE STRIPE CUSHION: Use 4 x 100g balls Rowan *Chunky Cotton Chenille* in light brown and 1 x 50g ball Rowan *Fine Cotton Chenille* in dark brown, 1 small ball medium-weight string in off-white, pair 4mm needles, sewing needle and pins, 50cm-square feather cushion pad

METHOD FOR THE STRIPE CUSHION (*worked in one piece*)**:** Using 4mm needles and 1 strand of light brown *Chunky Chenille*, cast on 80 stitches and work 61.5cm in stocking stitch. Change to string and work 2 rows reverse stocking stitch. Next, change back to light brown *Chunky Chenille* and work 4 rows stocking stitch. Change to string and work 3 rows reverse stocking stitch. Change to 2 strands dark brown *Fine Chenille* and work in stocking stitch until knitting measures 82cm from cast-on edge. Change to light brown *Chunky*

swatches : stripes

ALTERNATIVE STRIPES: Introducing stripes is an easy way to give colour or texture to your knitting, to use up scraps of yarn, or just to add interest. Regular or irregular; colourful, tonal or self-coloured; narrow or broad; textured or smooth – the stripe possibilities are endless.

Top left: Simply purling stitches in a new colour on the right side of a stocking stitch fabric gives an uneven, raised textural stripe. **Top centre:** Knitting single rows of reverse stocking stitch stripes at regular intervals on a piece creates a vigorous pattern. **Top right:** As a contrasting highlight on a cushion worked in rustic natural-coloured string add a square of soft fur-like knitted fabric with a line of metallic thread stitched through the centre. **Bottom left:** Broad, even bands of coloured stripes in different stitch patterns produce an effective crisp look. **Bottom centre:** Extra-wide deep tonal colours in cotton chenille make a strong contemporary impact when worked in stocking stitch and reverse stocking stitch. **Bottom right:** A simple raised stitch bar of seasonal colour highlights large contrasting blocks of knitted colour.

tassel throw : beaded fringe

Here is a new contemporary classic, a re-look at the traditional chenille tablecloth remembered from

the darkened parlours of ancient aunts. This one doubles as a throw for either bed or couch. It is

knitted in four long panels of alternating reverse-stocking-stitch and stocking-stitch squares. The

throw shown here is approximately 128cm by 111cm (50½in by 44in), but you can make it as small

or as large as you wish – just stop working the panel strips when you've had enough. It really

couldn't be simpler. A sumptuous material, in either cotton or viscose, chenille has its own particular

characteristics. On the plus side it has a pile like velvet, but unfortunately this pile tends to make it

'spiral', and it has no elasticity at all. So as a tip – always cast on your stitches with a size fatter needle

to produce a neat edge. Fringe the ends of the throw with lengths of chenille and thread on, at

random, simple silvered glass beads and you have a new heirloom.

how to make : tassel throw

FOR THE TASSEL THROW: Use 10 x 100g balls *Rowan Chunky Cotton Chenille*, pair 4¹/₂mm and 5mm needles, sewing needle and pins, crochet hook for making fringe, glass and wood beads

METHOD FOR THE TASSEL THROW: Using 5mm needles, cast on 48 stitches. Change to 4¹/₂mm needles and continue as follows:
Row 1: purl 12, take yarn to back of work between two needles and knit 12, bring yarn to front of work and purl 12, take yarn to back of work and knit 12. **Rows 2–16:** repeat last row 15 more times. **Row 17:** knit 12, purl 12, knit 12, purl 12. **Rows 18–32:** repeat last row 15 more times. Now repeat the 32 rows until 16 rows of 'squares' have been worked in total and knitting measures about

above left: To begin the fringe, pull doubled strands of yarn through the edge of the throw.

above centre: Then slip the cut ends through the loop and pull firmly to secure.

above right: Thread beads onto the fringe and simply knot to keep in place.

opposite: The richly textured tassel throw works well thrown over couch or table.

111cm from cast-on edge. Cast off using 5mm needles. Work another 3 panels in exactly the same way.

FINISHING: Sew the four panels together to form the throw, matching alternate squares. For the beaded tassels along the cast-on and cast-off ends, cut strands of yarn 30cm in length. You may find it easier to wind yarn around the length of a 30cm ruler and cut through both ends, to ensure that all the tassels are of a similar length. Hold 2 strands together and fold in half. Then, using a crochet hook, pull folded end through edge of work. Slip the cut ends through the folded loops and pull firmly to secure. Work a fringe sequence of doubled strands and single strands alternately. Thread beads onto single strands and knot in position randomly along the fringe.

floor cushion : stripe panels

Broad bands of fuzzy textures in subtle melanges of ivory and black via shades of flannel grey make

a contemporary textile for this luxuriously soft floor cushion. Strands of alpaca, bouclé and chenille

are mixed together to soften the tones and create new colours. By taking one strand of two

contrasting yarns and knitting them as one you are creating unique shades and textures from

standard yarns. The blurry stripe pattern on the cushion is enormously effective yet extemely easy to

knit. Combinations of 'rough' reverse stocking stitch and 'smooth' stocking stitch textures are used

for the irregular stripes. To keep track of which is the right side and which the wrong side of your

knitting, be sure to mark the right side when you work your first stripe. The cushion front is made

in three striped sections sewn together to form a square, and the back is worked in one piece in a

single colour. This is a perfect accessory in the living area for Bohemian styling in a modern setting.

how to make : **floor cushion**

FOR THE FLOOR CUSHION: Use 3 x 50g balls Jaeger *Alpaca* in cream, 1 ball in light grey and 1 ball in dark grey; 8 x 50g balls Jaeger *Persia* in ivory, 2 balls in mid grey and 1 ball in dark grey; 1 x 50g ball Rowan *Fine Cotton Chenille* in black; and pair 5mm needles, sewing needle and pins, 72cm-square cushion pad

COLOUR KEY: Each stripe colour is created by using two different strands of yarn together to make the following new texture and colour combinations:

- **A (off-white)** =1 strand cream *Alpaca* and 1 strand ivory *Persia* used together
- **B (light grey)** = 1 strand light grey *Alpaca* and 1 strand mid grey *Persia* used together
- **C (charcoal)** = 1 strand dark grey *Persia* and 1 strand black *Chenille* used together (will knit slightly thicker than other colours)
- **D (pastel grey)** = 1 strand light grey *Alpaca* and 1 strand ivory *Persia* used together
- **E (dark grey)** =1 stand dark grey *Alpaca* and 1 strand dark grey *Persia used together*

left: If the row is purled on the right side of the knitted fabric when a new shade is added, a broken colour line is created and a ridged texture is produced. New colours introduced in plain stocking stitch, however, produce stripes with smooth edges and smooth surfaces.

right: Measuring about 72cm (28½in) square when finished, this large luxurious cushion is knitted in soft yarn textures and tonal stripes (see page 125 for descriptions and specifications of the yarns used). The comfortable informal floor cushion is the new accessory for easy living.

METHOD FOR THE FLOOR CUSHION: THE BACK: With 5mm needles, cast on 101 stitches using A (see colour key). Work in stocking stitch for 72cm. Cast off.

THE FRONT: *(worked in 3 pieces)*: The front has two side pieces and one centre panel. *For each side piece,* cast on 25 stitches using 5mm needles and A. Work 18 rows A in stocking stitch, 18 rows B and 1 row A in reverse stocking stitch, 33 rows A in stocking stitch, 28 rows B and 1 row A in reverse stocking stitch, 33 rows A in stocking stitch, 18 rows B and 1 row A in reverse stocking stitch, and 17 rows A in stocking stitch. Cast off. Make the second side piece the same way. *For centre panel,* cast on 50 stitches using 5mm needles and D. Work 6 rows D, 6 rows C and 4 rows D in stocking stitch, 18 rows B and 1 row D in reverse stocking stitch, 3 rows D and 10 rows E in stocking stitch, (3 rows D in stocking stitch, 1 row C in reverse stocking stitch) 3 times, 8 rows D in stocking stitch, 28 rows B and 1 row D in reverse stocking stitch, 7 rows D in stocking stitch, (1 row C in reverse stocking stitch, 3 rows D in stocking stitch) 3 times, 10 rows E and 4 rows D in stocking stitch, 18 rows B and 1 row D in reverse stocking stitch, 3 rows D, 6 rows C and 6 rows D in stocking stitch. Cast off using D.

FINISHING: Sew in all yarn ends. Complete front of cushion by pinning 3 panels together with right sides facing and matching the wide B stripes. Sew the panel seams using a fine backstitch and 2 strands of cream *Alpaca*. With right sides together, pin the front piece to the back piece and sew around three sides, leaving the fourth side open. Turn right side out, insert the cushion pad and sew up the last side.

table runner : stripes and beads

Once only remembered as a strip of fabric sliding over your grandmother's sideboard, anchored only

by a glass fruit bowl, the image of the table runner has changed. It is now a desirable contemporary

homeware accessory, perfect for informal dining in or out of doors. A strip of texture and colour will

effectively set off and accentuate your 'top of the table' crockery, cutlery, glassware and linen. This

is a simple starter project, so easy and quick to make and to coordinate to your individual table

decoration and design. Knitting this runner in your chosen shades, from classic neutral tones to strong seasonal colour, is an easy way to 'ring the changes' and add instant fashion to your interior. It is knitted in natural-coloured string, but you could use cotton or linen yarn instead. Edged at each end with a simple border in tonal stripes, inspired by tea-towel patterns, it is further embellished with raffia and an eclectic mix of wood and glass beads for a rustic look.

how to make: table runner

22–26: stocking stitch using string. **Row 27:** purl using string to make a purl bar.

Continue in stocking stitch and string until work measures 33cm from last purl bar, ending with a purl row. Using dark olive, purl across next row to make a bar, then continue in stocking stitch until this olive section measures 25cm from the last purl bar, ending with a purl row. With string, purl across next row to make a bar, then continue in stocking stitch until this string section measures 33cm from the last purl bar, finishing with a purl row. To complete the table runner work from row 27 back to row 1 and cast off using raffia.

FINISHING: Thread beads onto lengths of fine string and attach along narrow ends of the runner. Then sew beads along third stripe from each end.

left A simple knitted textile to coordinate with tableware for informal dining.

top right: Match yarn to string weight by using several strands at once.

bottom right: Use fine string for threading beads.

FOR THE TABLE RUNNER: Use 1 skein ecru raffia, 6 balls medium-weight string for knitting, 3 x 50g balls Rowan *Cotton Glacé* in dark olive and 1 ball in light green, 1 ball fine string for attaching beads, pair 6mm needles, large sewing needle, assorted beads

METHOD FOR THE TABLE RUNNER: Using 6mm needles and raffia, cast on 45 stitches.
Rows 1–6: starting with a knit row, work 6 rows stocking stitch using medium-weight string. **Row 7:** purl using 3 strands light green cotton yarn to make a purl bar. **Rows 8–12:** stocking stitch using light green. **Row 13:** knit using string. **Row 14:** purl using 3 strands dark olive cotton yarn. **Row 15:** purl using dark olive to make a purl bar. **Rows 16–19:** stocking stitch using string. **Row 20:** knit using string to make a purl bar. **Row 21:** purl using string to make a purl bar. **Rows**

beaded cushions : linen or chenille

Opposites attract, so mix silk with linen, wood with metal – anything goes. Simple decorative touches add an innovative twist to these most basic cushions. To make the 'fold-over' cushion you just knit a long 'scarf' in your favourite yarn, fold it in half widthways, seam, bead the ends, stuff with a soft cushion pad and allow the excess fabric to flop over. The chenille reverse stocking stitch cushion is also decorated with beads, but only in the corners, and it has a simple overlapping back

opening. Your beading will be totally individual and unique – the only limitation is the strength of

your imagination. Scour second-hand shops and flea markets for old and broken bead necklaces and

vintage trimmings. Choose sumptuous textures in colours of comfort and warmth for inside or

natural flax or bleached linen for that special evening dining al fresco. Remember, if you want to

you can make your cushion to a special size with a minimum of effort (see page 124).

how to make : beaded cushions

FOR THE 'FOLD-OVER' CUSHION: Use 250g of very lightweight linen yarn and small amount in a contrasting colour, pair 3¹/₄mm needles, sewing needle and pins, assorted beads, 40cm x 30cm feather cushion pad

METHOD FOR THE 'FOLD-OVER' CUSHION: Using 3¹/₄mm needles and contrasting yarn, cast on 112 stitches. Knit 4 rows to make a garter-stitch edge. Using main yarn, work 101.5cm stocking stitch. Using contrasting yarn, knit 4 rows for garter-stitch edge. Cast off.

FINISHING: Gently steam work. Fold knitting in half widthways with right sides together. Sew two side seams using fine backstitch or running stitch. Turn right side out. Insert the cushion pad into the 'bag', and allow excess fabric to fold over and make a flap. Sew beads all along the open end at intervals. For fringe, thread beads onto separate lengths of yarn and knot in position. Sew 'strings' of beads at intervals around the garter-stitch edge.

FOR THE REVERSE STOCKING STITCH CUSHION: Use 3 x 100g balls Rowan *Chunky Cotton Chenille*, pair 4mm, 4¹/₂mm and 5mm needles, large sewing needle and pins, beads, 40cm x 30cm feather cushion pad

METHOD FOR THE REVERSE STOCKING STITCH CUSHION: With 5mm needles, cast on 62 stitches. Using 4¹/₂mm needles, work 68cm reverse stocking stitch, tying a coloured piece of yarn to the last and first stitch when work measures 21cm and 51cm, to indicate where to 'fold'. Cast off with 4mm needle.

FINISHING: Gently steam work. Fold knitting at the fold markers so that purl sides are facing and ends overlap in the middle. Sew side seams with fine backstitch or running stitch. Turn right side out. Thread beads onto lengths of yarn, not necessarily chenille which may be too thick. Attach bead decoration to two top corners. Insert the cushion pad.

opposite left: Strings of beads are attached along the edge of the 'fold-over' cushion.

opposite right: Bead clusters decorate the corners of the reverse stocking stitch cushion.

this page: The 'fold-over' beaded cushion is knitted in a fine linen yarn and the reverse stocking stitch beaded cushion in a thick cotton chenille.

swatches : beading

ALTERNATIVE BEADING: Whether your beads are wood, glass metal, stone, pearl or ceramic, round, oval or square, faceted or smooth, opaque, transparent, frosted or polished, there are many ways to use them to adorn your knitting. Here are some simple bead decorations that are sewn on, not knitted in. Play with contrasting textures and colours, mixing the beads at random or organising them in neat repeating rows.

Top left: Simple ribs in cotton ar set off here with tiny seed-like natural wood beads. **Top centre:** Strands of metallic bugle beads with natural coconut drops alternate with tiny beads knotted at intervals along strings. **Top right:** For this simple fastening idea, a leather string is threaded through a button on the inside of a chenille cushion and the ends are decorated randomly with glass and wood beads. **Bottom left:** Tonal beads in simple geometric patterns and motifs create an interesting border.

Bottom centre: Ordinary string threaded with raffia and rows of wood beads creates a rustic plaid. **Bottom right:** Randomly spaced between rows of purl bars, simple lines of glass beads produce a refined pattern on silk.

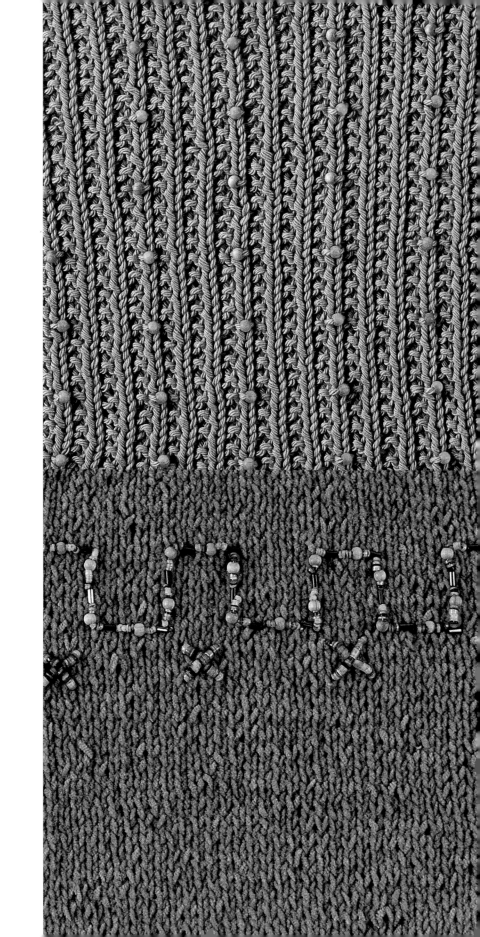

sleeping

squares throw : felted wool

This is it – the ultimate comfort blanket. And as an interior fashion statement it will give you an

instant home-decoration magazine look. You'll love it and it's fast to knit. Made in the lightest,

loftiest and most up-to-the-minute yarn ever, this large throw is warm, cosy and comfortable to the

touch. To make it, all you do is knit blocks of stocking-stitch and reverse-stocking-stitch squares and

sew the completed blocks together. The pattern of alternating square textures is similar to that of

the tassel throw (see pages 50–53), but the size of the squares and the feel of the yarn gives it a

completely different character. For the edging, you knit four long strips in stocking stitch and join

them to the outer edges of the throw, butting them together at the corners. This simple border is

left to naturally roll in on itself. Although it is a project you can pick up and put down, I guarantee

that you will want to finish it and won't let it languish in a bottom drawer.

how to make:squares throw

FOR THE SQUARES THROW: Use 35 x 50g balls Rowan *Chunky Soft*, pair 7¹/₂mm needles, large sewing needle and pins

METHOD FOR THE SQUARES THROW: THE CENTRE SQUARES: With 7¹/₂mm needles, cast on 60 stitches. **Row 1:** knit 30 stitches, then bring yarn to front of work between two needles and purl 30 stitches. Repeat previous row, so that 30 stitches are worked in stocking stitch and 30 stitches are worked in reverse stocking stitch, until work measures 30.5cm from cast-on edge. **Next row:** to make the check effect you must now purl the first 30 stitches and knit the next 30 stitches. Repeat the previous row until work measures 61cm in total from cast-on edge. Cast off. Make a total of 9 of these squares.

above left: The trim is made of long strips of stocking stitch, butted together at the corners, and is left to roll in on itself.

above right: The pattern of simple squares of stocking stitch and reverse stocking stitch.

opposite: Soft, textured yarn set off by crisp fresh linen creates a very modern look – plain and simple comfort. The finished squares throw measures 183cm by 183cm (72in by 72in).

TRIM: With 7¹/₂mm needles, cast on 5 stitches. Work in stocking stitch, slipping the first stitch and knitting the last stitch of each row to give neat, firm edges. Work 4 strips in this way, each 180cm long.

FINISHING: Sew in all ends by weaving along knitting not along edge. Lay each 'square' out flat and gently steam. Then lay out the 9 squares in a grid 3 squares wide by 3 squares deep. Pin the squares together, making sure that stitches alternate to make a pattern. Sew squares together by oversewing the seams on the inside. Pin a trim-strip to one side of throw so that strip extends 4cm past one end. Pin second strip in place all along next side, sewing one end to overlap and letting strip extend 4cm past other end. Sew on third and fourth strips in the same way.

felted sweater : an old friend

This is what I call an 'old friend' sweater. The kind that is always there for you – cosy to scramble

hurriedly into on chilly weekend mornings, to relax into when free from work, or to travel in as your

comforter – a timeless classic. Made oversized to fit all, it is worked in five easy rectangles of stocking

stitch – a back and front, two sleeves and a collar. Worked in a thick, soft felted yarn, the rectangles

grow fast on the needles. Side vents and a cowl neck are all that it needed to give a sense of style

to the very simplistic shape, and the outside seam details add a unique character. My one finishing

tip is to use a wool yarn in a matching colour for joining seams, since the loftiness of the felted yarn

can make it fray or separate when it is used for stitching. If you choose to make the felted sweater

in a soft neutral grey it will become a seasonal piece, in black a classic. But whatever shade you

choose, I'm sure you'll still be wearing it ten years from now!

how to make:felted sweater

FOR THE FELTED SWEATER: Use 17 x 50g balls Rowan *Chunky Soft*, pair 7^1/2mm needles, large sewing needle and pins

METHOD FOR THE FELTED SWEATER: BACK: With 7^1/2mm needles, cast on 62 stitches. Begin the ribbing with a right-side row as follows:
Rib row 1: (purl 2, knit 1) to last 2 stitches, purl 2. **Rib row 2:** (knit 2, purl 1) to last 2 stitches, knit 2.
Now work rib side vents integrally by keeping first 5 stitches and last 5 stitches on needle in rib (as set in first 2 rows) and stitches in between in stocking stitch until knitting measures 18cm from cast-on edge. Then work all 62 stitches in stocking stitch until back measures 42cm from cast-on edge. Place coloured strand of yarn at each end of last row for position of armholes. Continue in stocking stitch until back measures 68.5cm. Cast off.
THE FRONT: Work the front exactly as for the back.
THE SLEEVES (*2 the same*): Using 7^1/2mm needles, cast on 53 stitches. Work 2 rows of ribbing as for back. Then beginning with a knit row, work in stocking stitch until sleeve measures 46cm from cast-on edge. Cast off.
THE COLLAR: With 7^1/2mm needles, cast on 61 stitches. Work in stocking stitch for 21cm. Cast off.

FINISHING: Lay each piece out and gently steam flat. With wrong sides facing, pin front and back together at shoulders. Leaving neck opening in the middle, stitch 15cm at each side using yarn and a very fine running stitch – these seams will be on the outside of the sweater. Sew each sleeve in place in between markers using very fine running stitch and again with seam on outside of the sweater. Fold sweater in half at shoulder so that right sides are together and sew sleeve seams and side seams above 'vent' trim. Turn the sweater right side out. For the collar, pin and stitch the centre back collar seam so that the collar forms a ring. Then pin smooth side of collar to the inside of the neck edge, and sew collar into opening using running stitch and leaving seam to show on the outside as detail. Fold collar towards the outside, and turn back cuffs.

opposite left: A few stitches in rib on each side of the vents are just one of the details that give the sweater a sense of style.

opposite right: Sew the seams so that they show on the outside or are invisible on the inside as instructed.

this page: A functional yet fashionably felted oversize sweater. Your new best friend?

colour-block throw : tonal greys

Simply graphic, modern and minimal, clean and chic, this throw is an absolutely essential home accessory. Its refined elegance will add a touch of contemporary classicism to any of the comfort zones in your house. Knitted in four separate blocks of monochromatic colour that are stitched together when complete, the throw uses a soft extra-fine merino wool for three of the large squares and a contrasting bouclé texture for the fourth. Merino wool is a high quality yarn that is beautiful

to touch, so a joy to work with. And because it has a smooth surface and a subtle sheen, it gives great stitch definition – just the thing to add elegance to a simple design. A garter-stitch border is integrated into each square, so there's no trim to add around the edge later. Here's your opportunity to try out alternative yarns on an easy pattern. To really cosset yourself, what about knitting the throw in the noble yarns – alpaca, cashmere or angora.

how to make : **colour-block throw**

FOR THE COLOUR-BLOCK THROW: Use 8 x 50g balls of Jaeger *Extra Fine Merino* each in off-white, light grey and charcoal, and 5 x 50g balls Jaeger *Persia* in mid grey, pair 4mm and 4^1/2mm needles, large sewing needle and pins

METHOD FOR COLOUR-BLOCK THROW: THE MERINO SQUARES: Using 4mm needles and off-white *Merino*, cast on 176 stitches and work 6cm garter stitch (knit every row). Then begin with a right-side row as follows:
Next row (right side): knit to end of row. **Next row:** knit 13, purl to last 13 stitches, knit 13.
Keep repeating last 2 rows (so that 13 stitches at beginning and end of row are garter stitch and centre 150 stitches are stocking stitch) until work measures 74cm from cast-on edge. Now work 6cm garter stitch. Cast off.

above left: Three knitted blocks in extra-fine merino wool are highlighted by the fourth block in a fuzzy bouclé. The joined blocks form a throw that measures 160cm (63in) square.

above right: The integral edge of garter stitch provides a precision border to each square.

opposite: Relaxed and easy elegance, a simple throw to cover bed, chair or couch in the contemporary home.

Work 2 more squares in exactly the same way, but using light grey for one and charcoal for the other.
THE PERSIA SQUARE: Using 4^1/2mm needles and mid grey *Persia*, cast on 128 stitches and work 6cm garter stitch. Then begin with a right-side row as follows:
Next row (right side): knit to end of row. **Next row:** knit 9, purl to last 9 stitches, knit 9.
Keep repeating last 2 rows (so that 9 stitches at beginning and end of row are garter stitch and centre 110 stitches are stocking stitch) until work measures 74cm from cast-on edge. Now work 6cm garter stitch. Cast off.

FINISHING: Lay pieces flat and gently steam into shape. Pin the 4 squares together, making sure that all the edges match. Sew all seams using a fine running stitch.

button cushions : stitch textures

Choose from a variety of stitch patterns for this tailored cushion – smooth stocking stitch, or a

textured moss stitch, rib stitch or check stitch. And there's nothing stopping you from trying other

simple stitch patterns, like garter stitch, other rib stitch variations or even reverse stocking stitch. But

be sure to use a good quality yarn – the better the yarn, the better the finish. The pattern calls for

a merino wool, but alpaca or cashmere are also perfect for this project. For a more casual or rustic

environment, you could try a tweedy linen or string. A group of cushions in different stitches but the

same yarn and colour would look good on a bed, or in different yarn textures on a couch. Sew on

beautifully simple natural mother of pearl buttons in ivory or charcoal to add the perfect finish. Or,

hunt for wonderful individual buttons in second-hand shops or flea markets. This is the final detail

that really counts. Take a look at pages 86 and 87 for more button and yarn combination ideas.

how to make : button cushions

FOR THE BUTTON CUSHIONS: Use 6 x 50g balls of Jaeger *Extra Fine Merino* for each cushion, pair 3³/₄mm and 4mm needles, sewing needle and pins, 5 x 20mm buttons, 40cm-square feather cushion pad

STITCH CHOICES FOR THE BUTTON CUSHIONS:
STOCKING STITCH PATTERN: Knit 1 row and purl 1 row alternately.

MOSS STITCH PATTERN: Row 1: (knit 1, purl 1) to end. **Row 2:** (purl 1, knit 1) to end. Repeat last 2 rows to form the pattern.

RIB PATTERN: Row 1: knit 2, (purl 2, knit 3) to last 3 stitches, purl 2, knit 1. **Row 2:** purl 1, (knit 2, purl 3) to last 4 stitches, knit 2, purl 2. Repeat last 2 rows to form the pattern.

CHECK PATTERN: Row 1: (knit 5, purl 5) to end. **Rows 2, 3 and 4:** as row 1. **Row 5:** (purl 5, knit 5) to end. **Rows 6, 7 and 8:** as row 5. Repeat these 8 rows to form the pattern.

METHOD FOR THE BUTTON CUSHIONS: THE BACK: With 4mm needles, cast on 90 stitches and work 40cm in your chosen stitch pattern (see above), finishing with a wrong-side row. With the right side facing and starting with a knit row, begin the button band by working 10 rows stocking stitch, ending with a purl row. With the right side (or the 'smooth' side) of the knitting facing you and using 3³/₄mm needles, work a purl row across the stitches for a very neat 'folding' row. Change back to 4mm needles, and starting with a purl row, work in stocking stitch for a further 10 rows. Cast off.
THE FRONT: Work the first 40cm as for the back, finishing with a wrong-side row. Then with the right side facing and starting with a knit row, begin the buttonhole band by working

4 rows stocking stitch, finishing with a purl row. Next, work the buttonholes as follows:
Buttonhole row 1 (right side): knit first 8 stitches, cast off next 3 stitches, (knit until there are 15 stitches on right-hand needle after last cast-off, cast off the next 3 stitches) 4 times, knit last 7 stitches. **Butthonhole row 2:** Purl across row, casting on 3 stitches over those cast-off in previous row.
Work 4 more rows stocking stitch, finishing with a purl row. Using 3³/₄mm needles, work a purl row across the stitches. Change back to 4mm needles and starting with a purl row, work 4 rows stocking stitch, then work another set of buttonholes as before in line over the previous set. Work 4 rows stocking stitch. Cast off.

FINISHING: Lay the work out flat and gently steam into shape. Pin back and front with right sides together, and use a fine running stitch to join three sides, leaving the buttonhole side open. Next, fold the button bands in half along the purl-stitch row, and sew to the inside. Turn cushion right side out and sew on the buttons to correspond with the buttonholes. Insert the cushion pad and button up!

top left: Knit a double row of buttonholes. When the cushion pieces are joined, fold the bands to the inside.

bottom left: The rib pattern button cushion, with a chenille stocking stitch alternative worked with a single stripe.

centre left: Stitch the buttonholes together with buttonhole stitch and sew the buttons to the inside of the band.

opposite: Mixing alternative versions of the cushion adds style. Try it in other yarns for contrasting textures.

swatches:buttons

ALTERNATIVE BUTTONS: Think of buttons as not only functional fastening devices, but as prime decoration as well. They add character and stylish detail and can make or break your knitted garment or accessory. Take the time to look at the enormous variety of buttons that are available to you – horn, bone, wood, shell, nut, glass, ceramic or synthetic. As a simple tip, remember that buttons with sewing holes will sit more snuggly on stretchy knitwear than those with protruding shanks.

Top left: Natural horn buttons on textured bouclé. **Top centre:** Metal or metal-look buttons on tweed create a vibrant contrast. **Top right:** Coconut shell buttons have been used in many cultures, but now come mostly from Asia. They are shown here on knitted string. Use the reverse side to give a two-tone effect. **Bottom left:** Mother-of-pearl here picks up all the lights in a colour on silk. **Bottom centre:** Troche pearl buttons from Asia on merino wool. Cream or smoky grey shades go with all colours. **Bottom right:** Mollusc shell buttons work exceptionally well on textured linen.

child's blanket : ridged stripes

Here's a new hand-me-down for for the pushchair or cot, perfect for a child to cuddle up in, snug

and contented, for an afternoon nap. The blanket is knitted in a solid colour with thin garter-stitch

ridged stripes at the ends and a symphony of tonal blue and ecru textured stripes in the centre. For

the very simple coloured stripes, all you do is join in a new colour with each row, choosing the yarns

at random. The ridged texture comes from mixing one or two rows of 'rough' reverse stocking stitch

into the 'smooth' stocking stitch. Although the random stripes have an overall consistency, there's

no symmetry – so you can't go wrong with your knitting! Garter-stitch trim sewn to the finished

blanket adds stylish detail and secures the otherwise loose edges. Making this project can be a good

way to use up yarn left over from other knits. Why not try it in other colour schemes, substituting

the smooth cotton used here for different, more fuzzy fibre textures.

how to make : child's blanket

FOR THE CHILD'S BLANKET: Use 10 x 50g balls Rowan *Handknit D.K. Cotton* in ecru and 1 ball each in navy, ice blue and beige, and 1 x 100g ball Rowan *Chunky Cotton Chenille* in lavender, pair 3¼mm and 3¾mm needles, sewing needle and pins

METHOD FOR THE CHILD'S BLANKET: THE CENTRE OF BLANKET: Using 3¾mm needles and ecru *Handknit D.K. Cotton*, cast on 130 stitches. Still using the ecru cotton, work the first 48 rows of border as follows:
Starting with a knit (right-side) row, work 6 rows in stocking stitch (knit 1 row and purl 1 row alternately), mark the right side with a coloured thread, then work 2 rows in garter stitch (knit every row), 2 rows in stocking stitch, 2 rows in garter stitch, 6 rows in stocking stitch, 4rows in garter stitch, 8 rows in stocking stitch, 2 rows in garter stitch, 4 rows in stocking stitch, 4 rows in garter stitch, and 8 rows in stocking stitch.

Next, begin the textured stripe section of the blanket using 5 different yarns for the stripes – ecru, navy, ice blue and beige *Handknit D.K. Cotton*, and lavender *Chunky Cotton Chenille*. Work the stripes in a random pattern, changing the yarn on every row and randomly working a few rows in stocking stitch alternating with 1 or 2 rows in reverse stocking stitch (purl right-side rows and knit wrong-side rows). Work a total of 148 rows in stripes in this way.
Now knit the 48 rows of the final border in ecru *Handknit D.K. Cotton* as follows:
Starting with a knit (right-side) row, work 8 rows in stocking stitch, 4 rows in garter stitch, 4 rows in stocking stitch, 2 rows in garter stitch, 2 rows in stocking stitch, 2 rows in garter stitch, 8 rows in stocking stitch, 2 rows in garter stitch, 4 rows in stocking stitch, 4 rows in garter stitch, and 8 rows in stocking stitch. Cast off.

FINISHING: Sew in all loose ends of yarn. Lay work out flat and steam gently. Next, work the trim for the blanket as follows:
THE TRIM: Using 3¼mm needles and ecru *Handknit D.K. Cotton*, cast on 9 stitches. Knit every row for about 83cm – this strip should fit neatly along one long side edge of the blanket. Cast off. Make another strip the same length. Evenly pin one of these trim strips to each long side edge of the blanket and oversew in place. Then make another 2 strips in the same way, each about 72cm long – each of these strips should fit neatly along one short side of the blanket including the ends of the trim strips. Pin these strips to the top and bottom edges of the blanket and oversew. Sew the ends of the strips together where they meet.

top left: The top and bottom ends of the blanket have textured borders worked in a single colour. Purl rows create surface relief.

bottom left: Neaten the edges of the finished blanket by adding the garter stitch trim. Butt the trim ends together at the four corners.

centre left: When working the simple stripes at the centre of the blanket, join in yarns at will; the random use of colour adds energy to the design.

opposite: The solid-coloured borders and trim soften the energetic stripes. The finished child's blanket measures approximately 72cm by 90cm (28¼in by 35½in).

child's cushion : embroidery

Childlike outlines of flowers, cats, little houses and stars come to life on these denim-yarn cushions.

Use your children's or your niece's, nephew's or grandchild's drawings to inspire your simple,

innocent motifs. Or, record your own childhood memories in this fun and practical way. The denim

yarn used is hard wearing and playful and fades in the rough and tumble of everyday living. It is

great for children's projects and rooms. Accent an indigo denim-yarn cushion with ecru embroidery

motifs or an ecru denim-yarn cushion with the indigo. Keep the motifs simple and fresh and they'll

be easy to embroider in backstitch. An even easier way to embroider line drawings on knitting is to

outline the shapes in fine running stitch, then go back over the shapes with a second row of running

stitch filling in the spaces left on the first journey. Maybe your child would like to have a go at the

embroidery! It's a good introduction to the fun of stitching.

how to make: **child's cushion**

FOR THE CHILD'S CUSHION: Use 9 x 50g balls Rowan *Denim* in main colour (indigo or ecru) and 1 ball in contrasting colour (ecru or indigo), pair 4mm needles, large blunt-ended sewing needle and pins, 50cm-square feather cushion pad

METHOD FOR THE CHILD'S CUSHION: Using 4mm needles, cast on 100 stitches and work in stocking stitch until knitting measures 60cm from cast-on edge (this allows for shrinkage – *see below*). Cast off. Make another piece in exactly the same way.

FINISHING: The *Denim* yarn shrinks in length the first time it is washed, so before sewing the cushion pieces together they must be washed. First, loosely

above left: Embroidering your knitting is a very simple way of enhancing a design.

above centre: You may need to use two or three strands of yarn to make the motifs stand out.

above right: Frame the cushion front with an outline of bold blanket stitches.

opposite: Fill in backgrounds with widely spaced stars made up of simple straight stitches.

wind some of the contrasting yarn into a small ball or hank. Then wash and dry the knitted pieces and the small ball at the same time, carefully following the instructions on the yarn label. Lay the pieces flat and gently steam, pulling them into shape. Using a large blunt-ended needle and contrasting yarn double, embroider one piece with simple motifs in fine backstitch; the cushions shown provide some inspiration. If you like, work motif details with other simple embroidery stitches. After the embroidery is complete, pin the two cushion pieces right sides together and join three sides with a fine running stitch. Turn right side out, insert cushion pad and sew up the opening. Work blanket stitch all around the cushion using a single strand of contrasting yarn.

simple slippers : moss stitch

These are the sweetest soft baby slippers you'll ever see! They are so irresistible that even having to

work the simple increasing and decreasing techniques won't put you off. Make them as a baby gift

or knit an adult size for yourself or your partner. Hand-made gifts are the best, and these relaxed

indoor shoes with their pared-down design are sure to be treasured. The baby sizes can be knitted

in either a denim yarn or a simple cotton knitting yarn, and the two adult sizes in denim yarn.

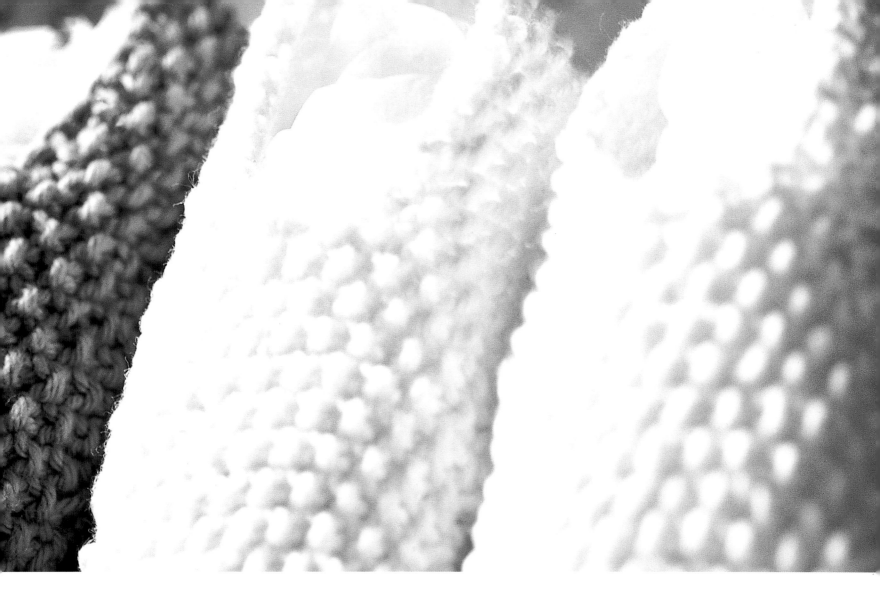

Although the denim yarn shrinks in length when it is first washed, this is no problem since the shrinkage is compensated for in the knitting pattern. Denim has an especially seductive feel and look, and gives the slippers extra firmness, so its worth that little extra care needed for washing and drying the pieces before stitching them together. Worked completely in beautiful textural moss stitch, these slippers are ideal for the bathroom or bedroom, or for lounging around the house.

how to make: simple slippers

FOR THE BABY SLIPPERS: Use 1 x 50g ball Rowan *Handknit D.K. Cotton* or 1 x 50g ball Rowan *Denim*, pair 3³/₄mm needles, sewing needle and pins

FOR THE ADULT SLIPPERS: Use 2 x 50g balls Rowan *Denim* in ecru, pair 3³/₄mm needles, large sewing needle and pins

MOSS STITCH PATTERN: *(over odd number of stitches)* **Row 1:** knit 1, *purl 1, knit 1, repeat from * to end. **Row 2:** knit the purl stitches and purl the knit stitches as they appear. Repeat row 2 to form the pattern.

METHOD FOR THE SLIPPERS: The pattern is written for the baby's size and the instructions for the adult's small and adult's medium follow inside brackets []; where there is only one figure, it applies to all sizes.

THE SOLES *(2 the same)*: Using 3³/₄mm needles, cast on 9 [11: 11] stitches and work 1 row moss stitch. **Baby version only:** Working the whole sole in moss stitch, increase 1 stitch at each end of next row by knitting into front and back of first and last stitch. (11 stitches on needle.) Work 9cm without shaping for *D.K. Cotton* and 10cm for *Denim*. Decrease 1 stitch at each end of row by knitting first 2 stitches together and last 2. **Adult versions only:** Working the whole sole in moss stitch, cast on 2 stitches at each end of next row. (15 [15] stitches on needle.) Work 21.5 [24]cm without shaping. Cast off 2 stitches at start of each of next 2 rows. **Both versions:** Cast off remaining 9 [11: 11] stitches in moss stitch.

THE UPPERS *(2 the same)*: Using 3³/₄mm needles, cast on 19 [41: 41] stitches. Working the whole upper in moss stitch, increase 1 stitch at end of next row by knitting into front and back of last stitch, then increase 1 stitch at same edge on the next 5 rows for the toe shaping. (25 [47: 47] stitches on needle.) Work 4 [10: 10] rows without shaping, finishing at straight back edge. Cast off 12 [23: 23] stitches in moss stitch at start of next row. Decrease 1 stitch at end of next row by knitting last 2 stitches together. Decrease 1 stitch at start of next row by knitting first 2 stitches together. Increase 1 stitch at end of next row by casting on 1 stitch after last stitch. Work 1 row without shaping. Cast on 13 [24: 24] stitches at end of next row. (25 [47: 47] stitches on needle.) Work 4 [10: 10] rows without shaping. Decrease 1 stitch at toe end on next 6 rows. Cast off remaining 19 [41: 41] stitches.

FINISHING: For denim yarn, wash and dry all parts of the slippers according to yarn label before sewing up to allow for shrinkage. Join straight edges at back of heel on uppers. Insert sole, pin around edge and attach using simple blanket stitch, easing in fullness around toe.

top left: Increase one stitch by working into the front and back of the same stitch (top), or several by casting on stitches (bottom).

bottom left: The adult slippers are knit in an off-white denim yarn. They are comfortable for the bathroom or the bedroom.

centre left: The slipper sole (left) and upper (right). Join straight ends of the upper before stitching on the sole.

opposite: Baby sllippers in shades of blue and ecru cotton yarn. Knit them in denim yarn or simple cotton yarn.

bathing

wash mitt : rustic sisal string

String provides the simplest and most basic yarn to knit in tonal colours from white, ecru and straw

to soft mellow golds. Rich in variety of texture, from fine cabled parcel strings, soft furry garden

twines to coarsely textured rustic sisal – string has endless possibilities for the interior. Its simplicity

adds an honesty to many homeware products all around the house from the living areas to the

bathroom, and from cushions and table runners to this authentic wash mitt. The wash mitt is worked

in sisal string in simple rows of knit and purl. It is a little hard on the hands to work with at first but

has a great effect on the body. Being naturally abrasive, it sloughs and softens. The wash mitt is very

easy to make, as it is knitted in one piece, folded over, then sewn together. This mitt measures 20cm

by 16cm (8in by 6in), but you could create a continuous long piece to use as a back scrub. Either, with

a piece of hand-made soap, would make a great gift for a friend.

how to make : **wash mitt**

seams. Fold the knitting half widthways, with the rougher side of work on the outside. Pin together before stitching if you wish. Use a running stitch to sew the side seams, leaving the end opposite the fold open. Now turn the mitt right side out. You may find it easier to push the 'corners' of the mitt to the inside first with the top of the knitting needle. If you like, make a loop for hanging the mitt by casting on 18 stitches (for a 25cm long cord) and casting them off in the first row. Sew both ends of the completed cord to the end of one seam.

ALTERNATIVE METHOD FOR THE WASH MITT: As an alternative you can work the mitt in two pieces 21cm by 17cm each and sew them together with the rougher side on the outside, working the seams on the outside as a detail.

left: String is the most basic of 'yarns'. A rich source of natural texture and colour, it is inexpensive and durable.

top right: Use a single strand (of the string) to sew up the seams.

far right: Rustic sisal is a natural abrasive to slough and soften the skin.

FOR THE WASH MITT: Use two balls of rustic sisal string available from most hardware stores (the coarser the better), the largest needles you can find, probably 10mm, large sewing needle

METHOD FOR THE WASH MITT: Cast on 12 stitches. Have a little patience, as the string will naturally twist and turn. Knit the first row and purl the next row. Just keep doing this – knitting 1 row and purling the next alternately – until your knitting measures 40cm. Cast off the stitches on the needle. You may find the sisal a little hard to work with and control. Try wrapping the string loosely around the needle; it will then be much easier to pull through.

FINISHING: Cut a length of string from the ball. Then unravel one strand of the string to use for sewing the

'bain' bag : cool cotton

This small, decorative project is knitted in a cotton yarn that is double-knitting-weight or medium-weight in thickness. It is worked in an attractive textured moss stitch and has a stocking-stitch hem at the top which is doubled over to provide a channel for a knitted or twisted drawstring. Because of its depth and sculptural quality, the single-row blue moss stitch stripe has the tactile look of embroidery. A separate panel for the simple cross stitch word is worked in stocking stitch and joined

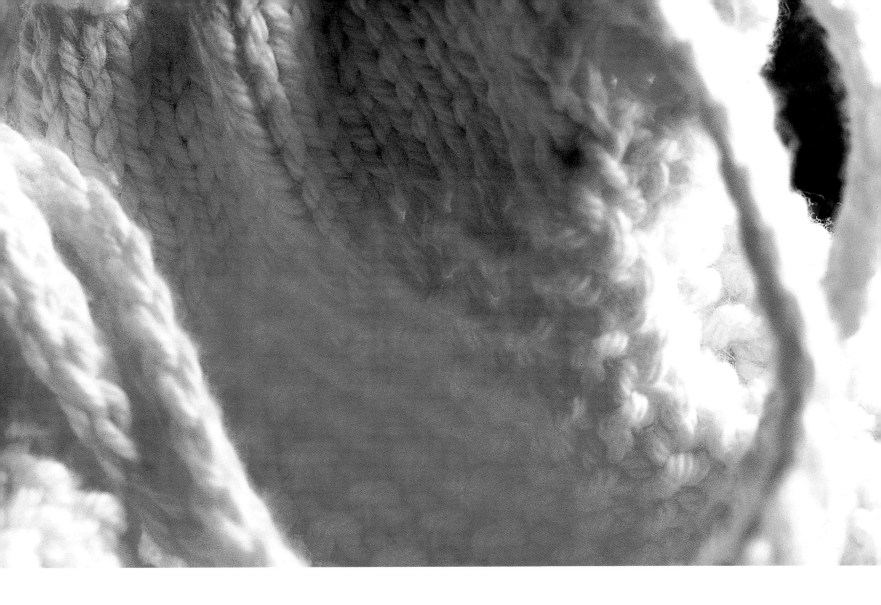

to the front. The distinctive word 'bain' has been chosen here for the embroidery, but you could stitch alternative words such as 'soap' or 'l'eau', or you may even wish to personalise the bag further with family initials or children's names, to hang in a row in the bathroom. Use this simple bag as inspiration for a larger bag for underwear or socks, or work a bag in a finer stocking stitch and embroider directly onto it. Have fun customising!

how to make: 'bain' bag

WORD PANEL: Using 3³/₄mm needles and ecru, cast on 30 stitches, work 7cm stocking stitch. Cast off. Using ice blue yarn double, embroider the word 'bain' in cross stitch or use your own design.

DRAWSTRING: Make a simple twisted cord 90cm long. Or, make cord shown by casting on 170 stitches and casting them off in the first row, then knitting into each cast-on stitch along the other side and casting off as they are picked up.

FINISHING: Press pieces. Stitch the word panel to the front, using a fine running stitch. With right sides facing, stitch back and front pieces together along the moss stitch only, using a fine backstitch. Turn right side out. Turn hem to the inside along the foldline and sew to the inside. Thread the drawstring through top of bag and knot ends.

FOR THE 'BAIN' BAG: Use 3 x 50g balls Rowan *Handknit D.K. Cotton* in ecru and 1 ball in ice blue, pair 3³/₄mm needles, sewing needle and pins

METHOD FOR THE 'BAIN' BAG: THE FRONT AND BACK (*2 pieces the same*): Using 3³/₄mm needles and ecru, cast on 50 stitches. Work moss stitch as follows:
Row 1: *knit 1, purl 1, repeat from * to end. **Row 2:** purl the knit stitches and knit the purl stitches as they appear. Repeat row 2 until knitting measures 5cm. Change to ice blue and work 1 row in moss stitch. Change back to ecru and continue in moss stitch until knitting measures 27cm from cast-on edge. Work 2.5cm stocking stitch, ending with a purl row. With right side (smooth side) of work facing, work a purl row to create a neat folding line for hem. Starting with a purl row, continue in stocking stitch for a further 2.5cm. Cast off.

top left: Leave the ends of the stocking stitch drawstring casing open when sewing the back and front together.

bottom left: Thread the drawstring through the top hem, pull the ends and tie them in a simple knot or bow.

right: The finished moss-stitch bag measures 27cm by 29cm (10½in by 11½in).

cuddle coat : soft chenille

This is absolutely what is says – a velvet-soft jacket to wrap around you when emerging from the bath or to cosset and cuddle you while just relaxing at home. It is knitted in chunky cotton chenille, which is naturally soft and absorbent and has a feel of luxury. Three-quarter sleeves and patch pockets add fashionable detail to this loose and comfortable knit. You may even decide it is too cosy to stay in the bathroom and make one in a classic elephant grey for chilly evenings out! So easy and

quick to knit in basic squares and no shaping! A characteristic of chenille is that it looks a little uneven in knitting, which I think is part of its charm. To add a beautiful refined quality to the finished piece, a simple tip has been followed – avoid ribbing. Traditional ribbed edges can look untidy in chenille, so here the edges have been kept deliberately plain with little vents and simple facings. The result is extremely neat, especially when offset with large natural troche pearl buttons.

how to make: cuddle coat

FOR THE CUDDLE COAT: Use 10 x 100g balls Rowan *Chunky Cotton Chenille*, pair 4mm and 5mm needles, 2 large buttons, large sewing needle and pins

METHOD FOR THE CUDDLE COAT: THE BACK: With 5mm needles, cast on 96 stitches. Change to 4mm needles and work in stocking stitch until back measures 45.5cm from cast-on edge. Place coloured thread of yarn at each end of last row for position of armholes. Continue in stocking stitch until back measures a total of 71cm. Cast off with 5mm needle. Mark 24 centre stitches at cast-off edge with coloured threads for neck opening.

THE RIGHT FRONT: With 5mm needles, cast on 61 stitches. Change to 4mm needles. **Row 1 (right side):** knit 8, purl 1, knit to end. **Row 2:** purl to last 9 stitches, knit 1, purl 8. Repeat last 2 rows until front measures 20cm from cast-on edge, ending with a purl row. **Buttonhole row 1 (right side):** knit 2, cast off next 4 stitches (3 stitches now on right-hand needle), knit 1, purl 1, knit 2, cast off next 4 stitches, knit to end. **Buttonhole row 2:** purl to first 4 cast-off stitches, cast on 4 stitches, purl 2, knit 1, purl 2, cast on 4 stitches over cast-off stitches, purl 2. Continuing in stocking stitch (with the single purl stitch stitch for facing foldline) for the whole front, work until front measures 40.5cm from cast-on edge, ending with a purl row. Make another pair of buttonholes as before. Then work until front measures 45.5cm from cast-on edge, and place coloured thread of yarn at armhole edge of last row for position of armhole. Continue until front measures 64.5cm from cast-on edge, ending with a purl row. **Neck shaping row (right side):** cast off first 25 stitches for neck shaping, knit to end. Continue on remaining 36 stitches in stocking stitch only until front measures same as back to shoulder. Cast off with 5mm needle.

THE LEFT FRONT: Work as for right front, but omit buttonholes, work purl foldline on opposite side, and cast off for neck shaping on a purl row.

THE SLEEVES (*2 the same*): With 5mm needles, cast on 80 stitches. Change to 4mm needles and work in stocking stitch until sleeve measures 30.5cm. Cast off with 5mm needle.

THE POCKETS (*2 the same*): With 5mm needles, cast on 28 stitches. Change to 4mm needles and work in stocking stitch for 16.5cm, ending with a knit row. Knit next row for foldline, then continue in stocking stitch until work measures 23cm in total. Cast off with 5mm needle.

THE COLLAR: Using 5mm needles, cast on 80 stitches. Change to 4mm needles and work in stocking stitch for 7.5cm, ending with a knit row. Knit next row for foldline, then begin with a knit row and continue for another 7.5cm in stocking stitch. Cast off with 5mm needle.

FINISHING: Sew in all ends on wrong side of knitting. Gently steam all pieces into shape. With right sides together and using backstitch, join shoulder seams, set in sleeves between coloured markers, then join side and sleeve seams leaving 7cm open at each lower edge for vents. Fold front facing-bands to the inside along purl foldline and slip stitch to inside. Matching the centre of collar to centre back neck, ease and sew collar in place. Fold collar to inside along purl foldline and slip stitch. Fold pocket flaps to inside along foldline and sew to fronts of coat. Finally, sew on the two buttons to correspond to the buttonholes and cuddle up!

opposite top: Two sets of buttonholes are worked on each side of a simple purl stitch, which creates a neat foldline for the facing.

opposite below: For neatness, oversew around the double buttonholes or use a blanket stitch.

this page: Soft velvet-touch cotton chenille is quick to knit and perfect to snuggle into after bathing or on waking in the early morning. (See page 125 for finished measurements.)

knitted baskets : moss stitch

Baskets are so easy to make – simply knit five squares! Worked in moss stitch for strength and

texture, and string for practicality and colour, these baskets are both useful and decorative. You can

sew the pieces together with the seams on the outside for a square box or turn inside out for a

rounded dish or basket shape. Experiment with different sizes, tiny and tall, or even try a lid to top

it off! Try indigo yarn and add starch to the final wash for extra rigidity. Use leather thonging or

raffia to create quite a different effect for another area of the house. These baskets will be functional in the bathroom, modern in the living area and fun in the playroom. There is no end to the designs you could attempt, for instance you could add single rows of colour to stripe and edge the baskets or decorate with simple embroidery. This is a great first knitting project for children to make for their treasures and trinkets.

how to make: knitted baskets

FOR THE SMALL BOX: Use 3 balls medium-weight string, pair 4mm needles, large sewing needle and pins

METHOD FOR THE SMALL BOX: With 4mm needles, cast on 19 stitches and work in moss stitch as follows: **Row 1:** knit 1, *purl l, knit 1, repeat from * to end. Repeat the last row until 30 rows have been worked from the cast-on edge and a square has been formed. Cast off in moss stitch. Make 4 more square pieces the same.

FINISHING: Sew in all ends. Wash pieces in warm water (40°C). If extra firmness is required, add starch to the water after rinsing. Pull pieces into shape and allow to dry flat; do NOT dry in a dryer. Using string, sew each of the 4 sides together with backstitch to make an open box.

top left: Pinch the seams together and backstitch in place, or use running stitch, then go back over the stitches filling inthe empty spaces (called double running stitch).

top right: Experiment with different sizes, yarns, textures, colours and even shapes.

opposite: Use in the bathroom for storing bath crystals, face cloths and guest soaps, or fill with the same to give as gifts!

Sew this joined piece to the base, leaving seams on the outside. Spray finished box with more starch if required.

FOR THE LARGE BOX: Use 5 balls medium-weight string, pair 4mm needles, large sewing needle and pins

METHOD FOR THE LARGE BOX: With 4mm needles, cast on 25 stitches and work in moss stitch as follows: **Row 1:** knit 1, *purl l, knit 1, repeat from * to end. Repeat the last row until 40 rows have been worked from the cast-on edge and a square has been formed. Cast off in moss stitch. Make 4 more square pieces the same.

FINISHING: Sew in all ends. Wash, shape and sew the 5 pieces together exactly as for the small box.

rag rug : mixed textures

Cotton, towelling, muslin, seersucker, string, ribbon, chenille – collect all your materials together

with colour and texture in mind for this rag rug. Use scraps of fabric and left-over yarn and the effect

will be random. But plan ahead and you can organise formal stripes, etc. For another look, try denim,

blues, indigo and chambray with crisp white or charcoal greys, black-and-white gingham, spot prints

or even ticking. Or mix natural and man-made materials together – experiment! Strips of different

fabrics will, of course, be uneven to knit, so if desired, use with chunky yarns or two or more strands

of thinner yarn to give a constant thickness. Knot the lengths together in a sequence of texture or

colour, or randomly. Then start to knit. When you're finished, push all the knots through to one side

and you have a choice of using the rug rough or smooth. But whichever, you have a beautiful texture

under foot. Instead of stocking stitch, try garter or moss stitch for extra texture.

how to make: rag rug

FOR THE RAG RUG: Use cotton fabric scraps in towelling, muslin and seersucker, as well as string, cotton ribbon and thick chenille yarn, pair 10mm knitting needles, large crochet hook

METHOD FOR THE RAG RUG: Cut the fabric scraps into strips approximately 2cm wide. Ply yarns together by selecting 2 or 3 strands of yarn and winding together as a ball. Now knot together various fabric strips and yarn to make a continuous length, and wind the length to create your own innovatively textured balls to knit with. Next, using 10mm needles, cast on 50 stitches. Work 1 knit row and 1 purl row alternately to form a thick stocking-stitch fabric, using each yarn combination as it comes from the 'balls'. Make more 'balls' as you need them. Continue

top left: The balls of knitting 'yarn' are made from a mixture of fabrics strips and thick yarns.

top centre: Knot fabric strips together with multi-strands of yarn textures to make a continuous length.

top right: Add a fringe across the top and bottom of the rug.

opposite: The knots on the reverse-stocking-stitch side of the rug create added texture.

until the knitting measures approximately 90cm, or the desired length, from the cast-on edge. Cast off.

FINISHING: Lay the work flat and gently steam into shape. You will notice that most of the knots go to the back or 'rough' side of the knitting. Either side can be used as the 'right' side. For the fringe, cut strips of fabric and lengths of yarn approximately 15cm long. You may find it easier to make consistent lengths by winding the yarn or fabric strips around the length of a 15cm ruler and cutting through both ends. Take a single strand, fold it double, then pull the folded end through the edge of the knitting from the wrong side to the right side with a crochet hook. Slip the cut ends through the loop and pull firmly to tighten. Trim if required.

yarn : characteristics & care

CHOOSING A YARN TEXTURE: The following yarn profiles will give you an idea of some of the pros and cons of knitting with various yarn types. Remember that the secret to getting the most out of any yarn is to experiment with it, trying out various needle sizes and seeing how it looks in different stitch patterns. Also, keep in mind that the texture of the yarn alters the look of the colours it comes in. (See page 125 for details about the specific yarns used in the projects in the preceding chapters.)

Alpaca yarn: Very light and as soft and warm as cashmere, alpaca yarn is usually less expensive than cashmere. It comes in beautiful subdued natural colours. Although it can be a little prickly, it is fine to knit with.

top left: Denim yarn is machine washable and and can be tumble dried. To finish denim yarn, you first have to shrink the knitted pieces by washing them to produce the hard-wearing and charateristically faded appearance (see opposite page for more about denim yarn).

top right: After washing knitted denim pieces, spin well and tumble dry. Then, if desired, air pieces for a final freshness.

Cashmere yarn: Cashmere is a noble fibre and the ultimate in luxury. It is ultra soft, light and beautiful to the touch. One drawback of cashmere yarn is that it is expensive due to the fact that the process of producing it is costly and lengthy. Also, the knitted fabric pills easily.

Chenille yarn: With its velvet-like pile, chenille requires a little patience to knit with. One good tip is to use a size smaller needle than you think you'll need for the main knitted fabric and use a size larger to cast on with.

Cotton yarn: Cotton has a natural look and is soft and cool to the touch. It is warm in winter and cool in summer. Cotton knitting yarns come in many versions –

matt or shiny, smooth or slubby and textured. Available in a wide range of colours, it is manufactured in many thicknesses as well, from very fine to very thick. On the down side, because it has no elasticity cotton can be harder to knit than wool until you've had a little practice with it. The finished knitted fabric is often weighty and can droop easily.

Cotton and wool yarn: Mixing cotton and wool in a knitting yarn creates the ideal combination. Wool adds elasticity for ease of knitting and stretchy comfort, and cotton adds elegance to the drape of the knitted fabric and a dry, smooth coolness to the touch.

Linen yarn: Extremely dry to the touch, linen has a subtle sheen and elegant drape. Linen blended with other natural fibres is beautiful. Very resilient, most linen knitting yarns can be washed in a machine and dried in a dryer. Linen creases but this can add to its charm. Some linen can be a little harsh next to the skin.

Silk yarn: Silk has a renowned natural sheen and an exquisite drape. It is luxurious and sensuous to the touch. Although it shows off knitted details well, it is not easy to knit with since, like cotton, it has little elasticity compared to wool. Some silk yarns can pill and sag.

String: The natural texture of string has a beautiful matt surface. It is economic and easily available in various thicknesses, from fine, smooth parcel string to medium-weight general purpose string to fat, rough sisal string. It is coarse and stiff to knit and can twist during knitting, but the attractive texture makes it worthwhile.

Wool yarn: Strong and flexible, wool yarn – like cotton – is warm in winter and cool in summer. Unlike cotton, however, it can be very lofty and fine, to lofty and chunky in thickness. Wool knitting yarn comes in any number of shades and in many textures, including tweed and bouclé. The very latest wool yarn texture is the fashionably felted variety. Its elasticity makes wool easy to knit and to knit quickly into an even, regular fabric. Smooth wools like merino create very precise, elegant and distinctive textures when knitted in raised stitch patterns, such as horizontal purl-stitch ridged stripes, vertical ribs, knit and purl checks, and fine moss stitch.

GENERAL CARE OF YARNS: The labels on most commercial yarns have instructions for washing (or dry cleaning), dryng and pressing. So for a project knitted in only one yarn, a quick look at the yarn label will tell you how to care for it. However, you may be working with several yarns in one piece, the child's blanket for example (see page 88), and in this case aftercare requires a little more thought. If one label suggests dry cleaning, then be sure to dry clean.

If in doubt about washing your knitting, it is a good idea to make a little swatch in the correct yarns and wash this to see if the fabric is effected by immersing in water or not. Watch out for shrinkage and stretching. If you are satisfied with the results, go ahead and wash by hand in warm water. Never immerse in hot water, this will 'felt' your fabric for sure, and you will not be able to return it to its pre-washed state.

Natural fibres such as wool, cotton and linen are usually better washed by hand. When hand-washing finished knitting, handle it carefully. Squeeze out excess water, never wring out. And rinse thoroughly until every particle of soap is squeezed out, as any left in will matt the fibres. Do not hang wet knitting; the weight of the water will stretch it out of shape. To dry, lay knitting out flat on top of a towel, which will absorb some of the moisture. Dry away from direct heat and leave flat until completely dry.

Check the yarn label before pressing your knitting. Most fibres only require a little steam, and the iron should be applied gently.

Look after your knits. Loose fibres can gather into balls of fluff on the surface. This is called 'pilling'. Cashmere and other luxury yarns are very prone to this. The fluff can be picked off or brushed over with sticky tape.

CARE OF DENIM YARN: Denim knitting yarn is very hard wearing, practical and machine washable. So it is great for children and adults alike. As with other indigo-dyed textiles, denim yarn will fade and age with wear and washing. Some of the dye will come off on your hands during knitting, but this washes off easily. Most of the excess dye is then lost in the initial wash. The knitted pieces will also shrink in length (but not width) during the first wash, which firms and tightens the knitting to a compact and robust fabric. This shrinkage is always allowed for in patterns that recommend denim yarn. Before you stitch knitted denim pieces together, wash them in the washing machine at 60–70°C (along with a small ball of yarn for seams). Dry the pieces flat, or tumble dry for a softer finish.

tension : tips

CHANGING THE SIZE OF YOUR KNITTING: You can change the width of your knitting to any size you want. First, knit a little bit of the proposed yarn. Then lay the knitting flat, smooth it out gently and count how many stitches there are to 10cm (4 inches) horizontally across the stitch widths. By multiplying the number of stitches per centimetre (or inch) times the desired knitted width, you can calculate how many stitches to cast on. For instance, if there are 15 stitches to 10cm that means there are 1.5 per centimetre. So if you want a cushion 50cm wide (1.5 x 50 = 75), then cast on 75 stitches. The number of rows per centimetre is usually less important, especially for simple projects – since you can just knit to the required length!

ACTUAL TENSIONS FOR PROJECTS: Because the projects in this book are mostly simple cushions, throws, etc., it is usually not essential to match your stitch size exactly to the one in the original project. In other words, if your cushion or throw comes out a little bigger or smaller than the one pictured it won't matter much. If, however, you want to change the size of your knitting or match an alternative yarn to the project, the original tension will help you with these processes, so they are given below:

PAGE 36 SIMPLE CUSHIONS: FINISHED SIZE: 50cm (19³/₄in) square. TENSION FOR COTTON CUSHION: 20 stitches to 10cm (4in) over garter stitch using 4mm needles and Rowan *Handknit D.K. Cotton.* TENSION FOR CHENILLE CUSHION: 15 stitches to 10cm (4in) over garter stitch using 5mm needles and Rowan *Chunky Cotton Chenille.*

PAGE 40 SEAMS CUSHION: FINISHED SIZE: 55cm (22in) square. TENSION: 11 stitches to 10cm (4in) over stocking stitch using 7mm needles and Rowan *Chunky Soft.*

PAGE 47 STRIPE CUSHION: FINISHED SIZE: 50cm (19³/₄in) square. TENSION: 15 stitches to 10cm (4in) over stocking stitch using 4mm needles and Rowan *Chunky Cotton Chenille.*

PAGE 52 TASSEL THROW: FINISHED SIZE: 128cm x 111cm (50¹/₂in x 44in). TENSION: 15 stitches and 23 rows to 10cm (4in) over stocking stitch using 4¹/₂mm needles and Rowan *Chunky Cotton Chenille.*

PAGE 56 FLOOR CUSHION: FINISHED SIZE: 72cm (28¹/₂in) square. TENSION: 14 stitches and 22 rows to 10cm (4in) over stocking stitch using 5mm needles and one strand Jaeger *Alpaca* and one strand Jaeger *Persia* together.

PAGE 61 TABLE RUNNER: FINISHED SIZE: 37cm x 127cm (14¹/₂in x 50in). TENSION: 12 stitches and 17 rows to 10cm (4in) over stocking stitch using 6mm needles and medium-weight string.

PAGE 64 BEADED CUSHIONS: FINISHED SIZE: The cushions each measure 40cm x 30cm (15³/₄in x 11³/₄in). TENSION FOR REVERSE STOCKING STITCH CUSHION: 15 stitches to 10cm (4in) over reverse stocking stitch using 4¹/₂mm needles and Rowan *Chunky Cotton Chenille.* FOR 'FOLD-OVER' CUSHION: 28 stitches to 10cm (4in) over stocking stitch using 3¹/₄mm needles and very lightweight linen yarn.

PAGE 72 SQUARES THROW: FINISHED SIZE: 183cm (72in) square. TENSION: 10 stitches to 10cm (4in) over stocking stitch using 7¹/₂mm needles and Rowan *Chunky Soft.*

PAGE 76 FELTED SWEATER: FINISHED SIZE: Finished sweater circumference is 116cm (45¹/₂in) and finished length is 68.5cm (27in). TENSION: 10¹/₂ stitches and 15 rows to 10cm (4in) over stocking stitch using 7¹/₂mm needles and Rowan *Chunky Soft.*

PAGE 80 COLOUR-BLOCK THROW: FINISHED SIZE: 160cm (63in) square. TENSION FOR MERINO: 22 stitches to 10cm (4in) over stocking stitch using 4mm needles and Jaeger *Extra Fine Merino.* FOR PERSIA: 16 stitches to 10cm (4in) using 4¹/₂mm needles and Jaeger *Persia.*

PAGE 84 BUTTON CUSHIONS: FINISHED SIZES: All the button cushions measure approximately 40cm (15³/₄in) square (not including button bands). TENSION: 22 stitches and 32 rows to 10cm (4in) over stocking stitch using 4mm needles and Jaeger *Extra Fine Merino.*

PAGE 90 CHILD'S BLANKET: FINISHED SIZE: Approximately 72cm x 90cm (28¹/₄in x 35¹/₂in). TENSION: 20 stitches and 28 rows to 10cm (4in) over stocking stitch using 3³/₄mm needles and Rowan *Handknit D.K. Cotton.*

PAGE 94 CHILD'S CUSHION: FINISHED SIZE: 50cm (19³/₄in) square. TENSION: 20 stitches and 28 rows before washing (20 sts and 32 rows after washing) to 10cm (4in) over stocking stitch using 4mm needles and Rowan *Denim.*

yarn buying:tips

PAGE **98** SIMPLE SLIPPERS: FINISHED SIZE: To fit baby, adult small and adult medium. TENSION FOR D.K. COTTON: 20 stitches and 28 rows to 10cm (4in) over moss stitch using 3^3/$_4$mm needles and Rowan *Handknit D.K. Cotton.* TENSION FOR DENIM: 20 stitches and 32 rows (before washing) to 10cm (4in) over moss stitch using 3^3/$_4$mm needles and Rowan *Denim.*

PAGE **105** WASH MITT: FINISHED SIZE: 20cm x 16cm (7^3/$_4$in x 6^1/$_4$in). TENSION: 7 stitches to 10cm (4in) over stocking stitch using 10mm needles and sisal string.

PAGE **108** 'BAIN' BAG: FINISHED SIZE: 27cm x 29cm (10^1/$_2$in x11^1/$_2$in). TENSION: 19 stitches to 10cm (4in) over moss stitch using 3^3/$_4$mm needles and Rowan *Handknit D.K. Cotton.*

PAGE **112** CUDDLE COAT: FINISHED SIZE: Finished coat circumference (buttoned) is 120cm (47in) and finished length is 71cm (28in). TENSION: 16 stitches and 24 rows to 10cm (4in) over stocking stitch using 4mm needles and Rowan *Chunky Cotton Chenille.*

PAGE **116** KNITTED BASKETS: FINISHED SIZE: Small box measures 12cm x 12cm x 12cm (4^3/$_4$in x 4^3/$_4$in x 4^3/$_4$in), and large box 18cm x 18cm x 18cm (7in x 7in x 7in). TENSION: 15 stitches and 25 rows to 10cm (4in) over moss stitch using 4mm needles and medium-weight string.

PAGE **120** RAG RUG: FINISHED SIZE: Depends on rags and yarns used. TENSION: Using 10mm knitting needles, stitch and row gauge will depend on rags and yarns used.

BUYING A SUBSTITUTE YARN: If you can, it is always best to use the yarn recommended in your knitting pattern (see pages 126 and 127 for Suppliers). However, if you do decide to use an alternative yarn – in order to find a specific shade or because you can't obtain the yarn recommended – be sure to purchase a substitute yarn that is as close as possible to the original in thickness, weight and texture so that it will be compatible with the knitting instructions. Calculate quantities required by lengths rather than by ball weights, and buy only one ball to start, so you can test the effect and the tension.

ACTUAL YARNS USED: The following is a list of the yarns used for projects in the book. The yarn characteristics given will be helpful if you are trying to find an alternative yarn. NOTE: The tensions given are all measured over stocking stitch, and the *ball/hank lengths are approximate.*

Jaeger Alpaca: 100% alpaca; a 4-ply alpaca yarn; 184m (201yd) per 50g ball; recommended tension – 28 stitches and 36 rows to 10cm (4in) using 3mm needles.

Jaeger Extra Fine Merino: a double-knitting-weight wool yarn; 100% extra fine merino wool; 125m (137yd) per 50g ball; recommended tension – 22 stitches and 30 rows to 10cm (4in) using 4mm needles.

Jaeger Persia: a medium-weight wool and polyamide bouclé yarn; 82% extra fine merino wool/18% polyamide; 100m (109yd) per 50g ball; recommended tension – 16 stitches and 26 rows to 10cm (4in) using 4^1/$_2$mm needles.

Rowan Cotton Glacé: a lightweight cotton yarn; 100% cotton; 115m (126yd) per 50g ball; recommended tension – 23 stitches and 32 rows to 10cm (4in) using 3–3^3/$_4$mm needles.

Rowan Chunky Cotton Chenille: a chunky-weight chenille yarn; 100% cotton; 140m (153yd) per 100g ball; recommended tension – 14–16 stitches and 23–24 rows to 10cm (4in) using 4–5mm needles.

Rowan Chunky Soft: a chunky-weight felted yarn; 40% wool/30% acrylic/20% alpaca/10% polyamide; 55m (60yd) per 50g ball; recommended tension – 11–12 stitches and 16–17 rows to 10cm (4in) using 6^1/$_2$–7mm needles.

Rowan Denim: a medium-weight cotton yarn; 100% cotton; 93m (101yd) per 50g ball; recommended tension before washing – 20 stitches and 28 rows to 10cm (4in) using 4mm needles. (See page 123 for special care instructions for denim yarn, which shrinks in length when first washed.)

Rowan Fine Cotton Chenille: a lightweight chenille yarn; 89% cotton/11% polyester; 160m (175yd) per 50g ball; recommended tension – 20–25 stitches and 36–44 rows to 10cm (4in) using 2^3/$_4$–3^3/$_4$mm needles.

Rowan Handknit D.K. Cotton: a medium-weight cotton yarn; 100% cotton; 85m (92yd) per 50g ball; recommended tension – 19–20 stitches and 28 rows to 10cm (4in) using 4–4^1/$_2$mm needles.

suppliers & acknowledgements

KNITTING YARNS: Full descriptions of the yarns used for the projects are given on page 125. Most of the projects in the book were worked in Rowan yarns; details for contacting Rowan Yarns and a list of selected stockists in the United Kingdom are provided below.

UNUSUAL 'YARNS' & ACCESSORIES: Other materials used for the projects, such as string, raffia, twine, beads and buttons, are widely available in ironmongers, craft shops and/or haberdasheries.

ROWAN YARNS WEBSITE
Contact the Rowan Yarns website for a complete list of stockists in the United Kingdom and for stockists in other countries.
www.rowanyarns.co.uk

ROWAN YARNS HEADQUARTERS
Rowan Yarns, Green Lane Mill, Holmfirth, West Yorkshire HD7 1RW, England.
Tel: 01484 681 881

SELECTED ROWAN STOCKISTS
Stockists in **bold type** are Rowan dedicated shops or departments, many offering professional help and mail-order facilities.

BATH AND NORTHEAST SOMERSET
BATH: **ROWAN AT Stitch Shop**, 15 The Podium, Northgate. Tel: 01225 481134
BRISTOL
BRISTOL: **ROWAN AT John Lewis**, Cribbs Causeway. Tel: 0117 959 1100
BEDFORDSHIRE
LEIGHTON BUZZARD: **ROWAN AT Needle & Thread**, 2/3 Peacock Mews.Tel: 01525 376456
BERKSHIRE
NEWBURY: Camp Hopson & Co Ltd, 6–12 Northbrook Street.Tel: 01635 523523
READING: **ROWAN AT Heelas**, Broad St. Tel: 01189 575955
SOUTH ASCOT: South Ascot Wools, 18 Brockenhurst Rd. Tel: 01344 628327
WINDSOR: Caleys, 19 High St. Tel: 01753 863241

BUCKINGHAMSHIRE
MILTON KEYNES: **ROWAN AT John Lewis**, Central Milton Keynes. Tel: 01908 679171
CAMBRIDGESHIRE
CAMBRIDGE: **ROWAN AT Robert Sayle**, St Andrews St. Tel: 01223 361292
PETERBOROUGH: John Lewis, Queensgate Centre. Tel: 01733 344644
CHESHIRE
CHEADLE: John Lewis, Wilmslow Rd. Tel: 0161 491 4914
HALE, ALTRINCHAM: Yvonne's Knitting Club. Tel: 0161 941 2534. Mail order. 24hr ansphone. Email: sales@internetwoolshop.com
CORNWALL
PENZANCE: Iriss, 66 Chapel St. Tel: 01736 366568
ST. IVES: Antiques, Buttons & Crafts, 3A Tregenna Hill. Tel: 01736 793713
WADEBRIDGE: **ROWAN AT Artycrafts**, 41 Molesworth St. Tel: 01208 812274
CUMBRIA
CARLISLE: Pingouin, 20 Globe La. Tel: 01228 520681
COCKERMOUTH: Silkstone, 12 Market Place. Tel: 01900 821 052. Fax: 01900 821 051. Mail order
PENRITH: **ROWAN AT Indigo**, 7 Devonshire Arcade. Tel: 01768 899917
DEVON
PLYMOUTH: **ROWAN AT Dingles**, 40–46 Royal Parade. Tel: 01752 266611
TAVISTOCK: Knitting Image, 9 Pepper St. Tel: 01822 617410
TOTNES: Sally Carr Designs, The Yarn Shop, 31 High St. Tel: 01803 863060
DORSET
BRIDPORT: Harlequin, 76 West St. Tel: 01308 456449
CHRISTCHURCH: Honora, 69 High St. Tel: 01202 486000
DORCHESTER: Goulds Ltd., 22 South St. Tel: 01305 217816
SHERBORNE: Hunters of Sherborne, 4 Tilton Court, Digby Rd. Tel: 01935 817722
STURMINSTER NEWTON: Hansons Fabrics, Station Rd. Tel: 01258 472698
WIMBORNE: **ROWAN AT The Walnut Tree**, 1 West Borough. Tel: 01202 840722

DURHAM
DARLINGTON: ROWAN AT Binns, 7 High Row. Tel: 01325 462606
ESSEX
CHELMSFORD: Franklins, 219 Moulsham St. Tel: 01245 346300
COLCHESTER: Franklins, 13/15 St Botolphs St. Tel: 01206 563955
MALDON: Peachey Ethknits, 6/7 Edwards Walk. Tel: 01621 857102 Mail order. Email: peachey-ethknits@ndirect.co.uk
SOUTHEND-ON-SEA: Gades, 239 Churchill South, Victoria Circus. Tel: 01702 613789
GLOUCESTERSHIRE
CHELTENHAM: **ROWAN AT Cavendish House**, The Promenade. Tel: 01242 521300
CIRENCESTER: Ashley's Wool Specialist, 62 Dyer St. Tel: 01285 653245. Mail order
GREATER MANCHESTER
DIDSBURY: Sew In, 741 Wilmslow Rd. Tel: 0161 445 5861
MARPLE: Sew In, 46 Market St. Tel: 0161 427 2529
HAMPSHIRE
ALRESFORD: Designer Knits, The Gable House, New Farm Rd. Tel: 01962 733499
BASINGSTOKE: Pack Lane Wool Shop, 171 Pack Lane, Kempshott. Tel: 01256 323644
LYMINGTON: Leigh's, 56 High St. Tel: 01590 673254
SOUTHAMPTON: Tyrrell & Green, Above Bar. Tel: 01703 227711
SOUTHSEA: Knight & Lee, Palmerston Rd. Tel: 01705 827511
TWYFORD: Riverside Yarns, Cockscombe Farm, Watley Lane. Tel: 01962 714380
WINCHESTER: C & H Fabrics, 8 High St. Tel: 01962 843355
HEREFORDSHIRE
HEREFORD: Singer Needlecrafts, 14 Maylord St. Tel: 01432 358986
HERTFORDSHIRE
BOREHAM WOOD: The Wool Shop, 92 Shenley Rd. Tel: 0181 905 2499. Mail order
WATFORD: **ROWAN AT Trewins**, The Harlequin, High St. Tel: 01923 244266
WELWYN GARDEN CITY: **ROWAN AT John Lewis**. Tel: 01707 323456

KENT
ASHFORD: Katie's Workbox, 15 High St, Headcorn. Tel: 01622 891065
CANTERBURY: ROWAN AT C & H Fabrics, 2 St. George's St. Tel: 01227 459760
GREENHITHE: John Lewis Bluewater. Tel: 01322 624123
MAIDSTONE: C & H Fabrics, 68 Week St. Tel: 01622 762060
ROCHESTER: **ROWAN AT Francis Iles**, 73 High St. Tel: 01634 843082
TUNBRIDGE WELLS: C & H Fabrics, 113/115 Mount Pleasant. Tel: 01892 522618
LANCASHIRE
ACCRINGTON: Sheila's Wool Shop, 284 Union Rd, Oswaldtwistle. Tel: 01254 875525. Email: sheilaswoolshop@compuserve.com
ST ANNE'S-ON-SEA: **ROWAN AT Kathleen Barnes**, 22 The Crescent. Tel/fax: 01253 724194
LEICESTERSHIRE
OAKHAM: **ROWAN AT The Wool Centre**, 40 Melton Rd. Tel: 01572 757574. Knitting up service available
LINCOLNSHIRE
LOUTH: Tudor Wool Shop, 13 Queen St. Tel: 01507 604037
LONDON - CENTRAL
EC1: Debbie Bliss, 365 St John St, EC1V 4LB Tel: 0171 833 8255
SW1: **ROWAN AT Peter Jones**, Sloane Square, SW1. Tel: 0171 730 3434
W1: **ROWAN AT Liberty**, Regent St, W1. Tel: 0171 734 1234
W1: **ROWAN AT John Lewis**, Oxford St, W1. Tel: 0171 629 7711
W2: **ROWAN AT Colourway**, 112A Westbourne Grove, W2. Tel/fax: 0171 229 1432. 24hr ansphone. Email: shop@colourway.co.uk
W4: Creations, 29 Turnham Green Terrace, Chiswick, W4 1RS. Tel: 0181 747 9697. Mail order
LONDON - NORTH & WEST
NW4: **ROWAN AT John Lewis**, Brent Cross Shopping Centre, NW4. Tel: 0181 202 6535
W13: Bunty's at Daniels, 96/122 Uxbridge Rd, West Ealing, W13 9RA. Tel: 0181 567 8729

LONDON - SOUTH
BARNES: Creations, 79 Church Rd, SW13.
Tel: 0181 563 2970. Mail Order
PENGE: Maple Textiles, 188/190 Maple Rd.
Tel: 0181 778 8049
MERSEYSIDE
LIVERPOOL: **ROWAN AT George Henry
Lee,** Basnett St. Tel: 0151 709 7070
NORFOLK
ROUGHTON: **ROWAN AT Sew Creative,**
Groveland Farm, Thorpe Market Rd.
Tel: 01263 834021
NORWICH: Bonds, All Saints Green.
Tel: 01603 660021
NORTHUMBERLAND
CORBRIDGE: The Fabric & Tapestry Shop,
Sydgate House, Middle St.
Tel: 01434 632902. Mail order
NOTTINGHAMSHIRE
NEWARK: Chameleon, 33–35 Cartergate.
Tel: 01636 671803. Ansaphone
NOTTINGHAM: **ROWAN AT Jessops,**
Victoria Centre. Tel: 0115 9418282
OXFORDSHIRE
BURFORD: Burford Needlecraft Shop, 117
High St. Tel: 01993 822136. Mail order
OXFORD: **ROWAN AT Rowan,**102
Gloucester Green. Tel: 01865 793366.
24hr ansphone
SHROPSHIRE
SHREWSBURY: **ROWAN AT House of
Needlework,** 11 Wyle Cop.
Tel: 01743 355533 (formerly Osa)
SOMERSET
BURNHAM-ON-SEA: The Woolsack, 7
College St. Tel: 01278 784443
GLASTONBURY: Penny Juniors, 40 High St.
Tel: 01458 831974
TAUNTON: Hayes Wools, 150 East Reach.
Tel: 01823 284768. Mail order
YEOVIL: Enid's Wool & Craft Shop, Church
St. Tel: 01935 412421
SUFFOLK
BURY ST EDMUNDS: **ROWAN AT Jaycraft,**
78 St John's St. Tel: 01284 752982
IPSWICH: Spare Moments, 13 Northgate St.
Tel: 01473 259876
SURREY
BANSTEAD: Maxime Wool & Craft Shop,
155 High St. Tel: 01737 352798

KINGSTON: **ROWAN AT John Lewis,**
Wood St. Tel: 0181 547 3000
GUILDFORD: **ROWAN AT Army & Navy,**
High St. Tel: 01483 568171
EAST SUSSEX
BATTLE: Battle Wool Shop, 2 Mount St.
Tel: 01424 775073
BRIGHTON: C & H Fabrics, 179 Western
Rd. Tel: 01273 321959
EASTBOURNE: C & H Fabrics, 82/86
Terminus Rd. Tel: 01323 410503
EAST HOATHLEY (NR UCKFIELD): The Wool
Loft, Upstairs at Clara's, 9 High St.
Tel: 01825 840339. Mail order.
Email: Claras@netway.co.uk
LEWES: **ROWAN AT Kangaroo,** 70 High
St. Tel: 01273 478554
WEST SUSSEX
ARUNDLE: **ROWAN AT David's Needle-
Art,** 37 Tarrant St. Tel: 01903 882761
BURGESS HILL: The Fabric Shop, 29 The
Martlets. Tel: 01444 236688. Mail order
CHICHESTER: C & H Fabrics, 33/34 North
St. Tel: 01243 783300
HORSHAM: The Fabric Shop, 62 Swan
Walk. Tel: 01403 217945
SHOREHAM BY SEA: **ROWAN AT
Shoreham Knitting,** 19 East St.
Tel: 01273 461029. Fax: 01273 465407.
Email: skn@sure-employ.demon.co.uk
WORTHING: **ROWAN AT The Fabric Shop,**
55 Chapel Rd. Tel: 01903 207389
TEESIDE
HARTLEPOOL: Bobby Davison, 101 Park Rd.
Tel: 01429 861300.
Email: mail@woolsworldwide.com
TYNE & WEAR
GATESHEAD: **ROWAN AT House of
Fraser,** Metro Centre. Tel: 0191 493 2424
NEWCASTLE UPON TYNE: **ROWAN AT
Bainbridge,** Eldon Square. Tel: 0191 232 5000
NEWCASTLE UPON TYNE: **ROWAN AT
Fenwick Limited,** 39 Northumberland St.
Tel: 0191 232 5100
WARWICKSHIRE
WARWICK: Warwick Wools, 17 Market
Place. Tel: 01926 492853
WEST MIDLANDS
BIRMINGHAM: **ROWAN AT Rackhams,**
Corporation St. Tel: 0121 236 3333

SOLIHULL: Stitches, 355 Warwick Road,
Olton. Tel: 0121 706 1048
WOLVERHAMPTON: **ROWAN AT Beatties,**
71–78 Victoria St. Tel: 01902 422311
WILTSHIRE
CALNE: Handi Wools, 3 Oxford Rd.
Tel: 01249 812081
SALISBURY: Stitches, Cross Keys Chequer.
Tel: 01722 411148. Mail order
WORCESTERSHIRE
KIDDERMINSTER: Woolwise, 10 Lower Mill
St. Tel: 01562 820279
NORTH YORKSHIRE
HELMSLEY: **ROWAN AT Tapestry Garden,**
2 Castlegate. Tel: 01439 771300
SETTLE: Ancient & Modern, 39 Duke St.
Tel: 01729 824298
WHITBY: **ROWAN AT Bobbins,**
Wesley Hall, Church St.
Tel/fax: 01947 600585.
Email: bobbins@globalnet.co.uk
YORK: **ROWAN AT Craft Basics,**
9 Gillygate. Tel: 01904 652840
SOUTH YORKSHIRE
SHEFFIELD: ROWAN AT Cole Brothers,
Barkers Pool. Tel: 0114 2768511
WEST YORKSHIRE
HEBDEN BRIDGE: **ROWAN AT Attica,**
2 Commercial St. Tel: 01422 844327
HOLMFIRTH: **ROWAN AT Up Country,**
6 Market Walk. Tel/fax: 01484 687803.
Email: gpaul@upco.u-net.com
WALES
CARDIFF: **ROWAN AT David Morgan
Ltd,** 26 The Hayes. Tel: 01222 221011
CONWY: Ar-y-Gweill, 8 Heol Yr Orsaf,
Llanrwst. Tel: 01492 641149
FISHGUARD: Jane's of Fishguard, 14 High
St. Tel: 01348 874443
SWANSEA: Mrs Mac's, 2 Woodville Rd,
Mumbles. Tel: 01792 369820
SCOTLAND
ABERDEEN: John Lewis, George St.
Tel: 01224 625000
BEAULY: Linda Usher, 50 High St.
Tel: 01463 783017
CASTLE DOUGLAS: Needlecraft, 201 King St.
Tel: 01556 503606
CRIEF: Lint Mill Knitwear, 1 Dunira St,
Comrie. Tel: 01764 670300

EDINBURGH: **ROWAN AT John Lewis,**
St James Centre. Tel: 0131 556 9121
EDINBURGH: **ROWAN AT Jenners,**
48 Princes St. Tel: 0131 225 2442
EDINBURGH: **ROWAN AT Wooly
Mammoth,** 17 Jeffrey St, Off the Royal
Mile. Tel/fax: 0131 557 5025.
Email: mammoth@ednet.co.uk
GLASGOW: John Lewis, Buchanan Galleries.
Tel: 0141 353 6677
HUNTLY: **ROWAN AT Not Just Wool,**
9 Bogie St. Tel: 01466 799045
ISLE OF ARRAN: Trareoch Craft Shop,
Balmichael Visitors Centre, Shiskine.
Tel: 01770 860515
ISLE OF SKYE: Di Gilpin, The Old Mission
Hall, Struan Workshop, Struan.
Tel: 01470 572 284
LANARK: Strands, 8 Bloomgate. Tel: 01555
665757. Mail order
LINLITHGOW: Nifty Needles, 56 High St.
Tel: 01506 670435
LONGNIDDRY: Longniddry Post Office, 29a
Links Rd. Tel: 01875 852894
SHETLAND ISLANDS: Wimberry, Gardens,
Skeld. Tel: 01595 860371. Mail order

AUTHOR'S ACKNOWLEDGEMENTS

To a very special team of people, who have each contributed a unique skill, and for their creative spirit, inspiration, dedication, patience, enthusiasm, endless support and that special artistic 'eye'.

With warmest thanks to **Kate Kirby, Susan Berry, Debbie Mole, John Heseltine, Stephen Sheard, Sally Harding, Sarah Phillips, Sally Lee, Hannah Davis, Wendy, Lyndsay** and **Kim at Rowan,** and **my daughter Bella** for, well, just about everything!

And a heartfelt thank you to all those anonymous women who have knitted, stitched and created, whose work I have discovered in flea markets and jumble sales all over the world and whose love and soul were stitched and worked into every fibre. Many of these women had no formal outlet for their work, just passion for their crafts. They continue to be a constant source of ideas and inspiration.

index